Below
MANCHESTER

Keith Warrender

2

Below
MANCHESTER

KEITH WARRENDER

Willow
PUBLISHING

First published 2009 by Willow Publishing

Willow Publishing
36 Moss Lane, Timperley
Altrincham, Cheshire WA15 6SZ

ISBN 978-0-946361-42-7

Book designed by Keith Warrender

Printed by the Buxton Press

Title page photograph: Guardian Apparatus tunnel no.7 January 1956

Dedicated to my mother

CONTENTS

Warning

Referral to any underground area or passage in this book does not imply or grant public right of entry. Willow Publishing and the author accept no liability for death, injuries or prosecution incurred through either authorised or unauthorised access to places mentioned in this book. Unless otherwise stated, all the existing subterranean areas included in the book are regarded as dangerous and closed to the public, and not to be entered, under any circumstances, without written official permission, without safety training, and under supervision.

FOREWORD

Fred Fielder
MBE FRGS
Radio Presenter

I first became interested in underground Manchester back in the Orwellian year of 1984. I had heard so many rumours about a so called underground city and Victorian shops still in-situ, so to speak, so I decided to investigate further. At first it was like 'the Indian rope trick' - everybody had heard about it but nobody had actually seen it!

Four friends and myself started to 'dig' for information and it wasn't long before the five of us assembled in the city centre one glorious sunny Saturday morning. So began 'The Orpheus Project'. I remembered as a young boy, the statue of Oliver Cromwell (now situated in Wythenshawe Park) with his back to Manchester Cathedral in the 1950s. I also remember descending steps with my Dad to the most wonderful white glazed tiled and mahogany public convenience I had ever seen. These underground toilets were shrouded by railings to stop revellers accidentally falling in after a late night foray at the nearby Yates Wine Lodge.

We began our first adventure underground which took us through a labyrinth of tunnels heading north, south, east and west, oh yes, we had a compass and ordnance survey map to correspond with the surface in relation to where we were underground. There were numerous peeling signs saying this way to shelter C, another sign saying 'no perambulators beyond this point'. We concluded this to be one massive public air raid shelter and to my first surprise we discovered the old tile and mahogany toilets covered in years of cobwebs and dust, but everything still intact. The corridors twisted and turned and after a while we came upon an old steel ladder fixed into the wall, a mixture of bonded brickwork and natural red sandstone. We ascended, one by one, and the warm fresh air flooded in, and then our next surprise, the click, click of stilleto heeled ladies. Where were we? I put my head up to the surprise of a passing female and recognised we were close to Manchester Cathedral.

We used to look forward to our Saturday morning jaunts. At the time I was working as a civil servant and used to relate my adventures to a staff room of colleagues who became avid listeners. I would emphasise to readers this was over twenty five years ago, and access we gained to these places has long since been removed and should not to be attempted today.

I once owned Knoll House on Bury New Road, an old timber-framed property that had originally been in Market Street and moved in the 1820s. It had been the residence of Chevalier Lafosse a pioneer in photographic portrait techniques, and the Marks family who co-founded the M&S stores. In the cellar I found a well with clear water, and towards the frontage of Bury New Road it seemed the brickwork had collapsed. On closer inspection, I discovered there was a tunnel. I found that it led all the way into Manchester, passing under the Grove Inn and Boddington's Brewery, and then in the direction of Walker's Croft graveyard under Victoria Station.

Now, fast forward to 2008 and it is brought to my attention that a book called *Underground Manchester* was on sale. Enter Keith Warrender, the author, who got in touch with me for my opinions on the subterranean phenomena after many people who listened to my radio programme had told him that I used to reminisce about my Orpheus Project on air.

We met one Tuesday lunchtime in Manchester's China Town. After listening to him I could see he was on the level and he even brought me a copy of *Underground Manchester* - book one - signed of course to a 'fellow tunneller'. I read the book and found it both factual and interesting. Kindred spirits, at last someone who had seen the things I had seen first hand. So good on you Keith - keep tunnelling, sifting and delving.

INTRODUCTION

In this second book on the subject, I include many new underground sites, as well as returning to places where there is more to tell - hence the subtitle of 'going deeper'. Wherever you are in the centre of the city, you are either standing directly over or are close to something of interest underground - and I am not referring to drains and sewers! Although even these hold a fascination for some, and a sense of pride for those who maintain them.

Building a telephone duct below Brown Street, February 1927

I knew I had a popular subject on my hands after that memorable day in April 2008 when so many people came to hear my talk on underground Manchester at Central Library. They queued in the corridor and others seeing the crowds just turned back. The meeting room was nowhere near big enough and I went through the presentation twice, going hoarse in the process of trying to make myself heard in the long narrow room. Those who did not make the talks hopefully got to hear it at the Friends' Meeting House on Mount Street a few weeks later. Around 190 people came along for that - clearly this mix of local history and mystery attracts much interest.

This book is intended to complement the first volume, and I do not generally go over the same information so, naturally, I would recommend you read 'Underground Manchester' as well.

It is fitting that on the seventieth anniversary of the last World War, a substantial part of this book is about the Manchester citizens' efforts to find safety below ground. The story of the once top-secret control centres, and the conditions in the public air raid shelters is fascinating. This time the book is in full colour so that the photographs are the next best thing to actually being down in the tunnels. While on the subject of photographs, I should also mention how few have survived from the files of newspapers. It is very sad that many important old photographs were simply thrown out because there was no space for them and no-one thought to send them to a public archive or library. Therefore I have had to take photographs directly from the pages of newspapers, which means that some are not of the best quality, but it is the best that could be done, and they are too vital to leave out.

As in 'Underground Manchester', I have included 'over-ground' information where it seemed appropriate. For example, the history of the Victoria Arches would have been incomplete if I had not included the fate of the lifeboat made there, or covered the rise and fall of the steamer excursion service from the landing stages.

Research into this subject is both exciting and frustrating. You never know what you are going to find, or what somebody is going to tell you after a talk. However, it is a topic that can send you on 'wild-goose chases', and some individuals and organisations can be unco-operative.

But as I go deeper into the subject, I realise there is so much more to find out. Even after writing a second volume, there are many other sites and accounts I know of, which I have still to investigate.

I am grateful to Fred Fielder and Dr Sandra Hayton for their contributions. I know that Fred and his associates generated a lot of interest on subterranean matters on his BBC Radio programme. They discovered underground routes nearly thirty years ago that seem to be closed to today's explorers.

Once this area below Market Place was used as a shooting gallery and for skittles, and then later converted into a cheese store for Goulburn's

Sandra brings an authoritative look to the subject of the below-ground homes in the city. My thanks, as before, to everyone who has shared what they know with me. If you know anything which may be of interest, please don't hesitate to contact me.

Once again I should remind readers, that these underground places are not be entered without official permission.

I hope you will enjoy this latest look below the streets of Manchester

KEITH WARRENDER, October 2009

EVENING CHRONICLE

A tunneller's memories

Charlie Coyle is a rarity; he is a former tunneller who has lived into old age. The dangers and diseases associated with this profession have taken their toll on many of his fellow tunnellers. Charlie remembers how three men working next to him were killed when a railway skip fell onto them. So many in the industry met early deaths from the inhalation of dust and engine fumes in the confined spaces. Others have been maimed and injured in accidents with machinery or suffered from 'the bends' after working under com-pressed air conditions.

Like most tunnel workers, he comes from Donegal. The county's work-force kept all this compara-tively well-paid work for itself for several generations, until recently, when 'incomers' from the west of Ireland have begun to take more of the jobs. Another group of workers involved are the Poles, whom Charlie describes as hard workers.

Charlie worked on Manchester tunnels but began in the 1950s in Perthshire, Scotland working on the hydro-electric schemes to run water from the lakes. Two local projects in which he was involved were the construction of a 10ft-high sewer tunnel at Mill Street, near Manchester City's stadium, and the refurbishment of a drain in St Ann's Square. He also worked on a mile-long tunnel at Snow Hill, Birmingham, which may have been part of the city's top secret 'Anchor Exchange' network.

On a good day, tunnellers could create 12 ft of tunnel. Every 2 ft they would install a steel rib to hold the sandstone in place. If the stone work was unstable, they would freeze it to prevent it from collapsing. On other occasions the ends of the tunnel were locked and compressed air used to prevent dampness. Explosives would penetrate into 3ft of rock.

One important reason for Charlie's longevity - he left tunnelling to work in the building industry, but he has good memories of the below-ground-work and his work mates.

Charlie still has the tunneller's tools - a drill, and a machine-driven spade.

Subways under the Co-op

Between Balloon Street and Miller Street there is much of interest below the Co-op buildings, including a system of subways, an air raid shelter entrance, and 'Cold War' refuges. The Metro system passes over three tunnels along Balloon Street. They once connected the Hanover and Federation buildings with the Co-op properties on the south side of the street. Subway (1) is from the sub-basement of the Packing department to the old Drapery department bounded by Garden Street and Dantzic Street. Subway (2), also from the Packing section, led to the Boot department. Subway (3) from the block containing the board room, offices, dining room and the Mitchell memorial hall, ran to the Furnishing department. Another subway (4) goes under Hanover Street to link the old Bank building with the Hanover building. Subway (5) with two adjoining conveyor ducts, joins E Block with the Federation building,under Federation Street.

Closed off link (2) under Balloon Street

13

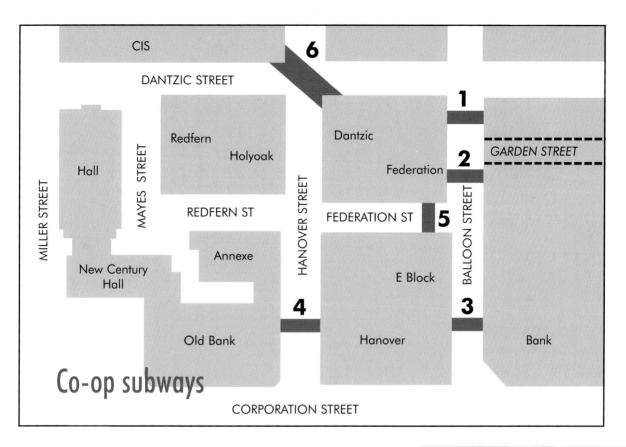

The Co-op buildings were built from c1905 to 1937. Most of these passageways are to be seen on 1929 plans, so they clearly pre-date any war-time preparations.

The tiled subways provided a safe and secure route for the transportation of goods and possibly money between the CWS buildings. Today, two of the Balloon Street subways are blocked off on the southern edge, and the third is not accessible from the doorway in the Federation building. The widest was the route to the old Woollen and Drapery department on Garden Street. However, the tunnel has become a store for assorted pieces of masonry and other items.

Above: Masonry stored in the subway (1)

Opposite page: Arched tunnel (1) under Balloon Street, indicated on old plans as 'conveyor subway'.

The routes under Federation Street and Hanover Street are still in staff use, and there is also a connecting passage between New Century Hall and the old Bank building. It should be noted that there is strict security in these places and they can only be accessed by staff.

This page and
opposite: conveyor
subways under
Federation Street

To go below the Co-op site is to enter a different world, with many reminders of its past use. Ray Lyons, my patient guide on several occasions, showed me the empty walk-in safe in the Bank building, and the 'lost world' of the old drapery department in E Block. He led me through room upon room of old company records which hopefully will one day be archived.

A later subway (6) can be seen under the Dantzic building. This was the route under Dantzic Street to the new Drapery building bounded by Dantzic Street and Mayes Street. The eight-storey high building which was under construction by 1938 had a bomb-blast shelter in the sub-basement for the 4,500 CWS employees and customers. In press publicity it was described as being well protected, 40ft below ground and surrounded by walls and a ceiling of 5ft reinforced concrete. Within the shelter, it was sub-divided into a series of 16ft wide bays. There were six entrances into the shelter and numerous staircases to prevent overcrowding.

Left: Subway (3) under Balloon Street

Top: Ray Lyons and the safe in the Old Bank building

Below: Ledgers stored in the same building

Opposite: Plan of the air raid shelter below the new drapery building, and elevation showing the shelters deep below

25488

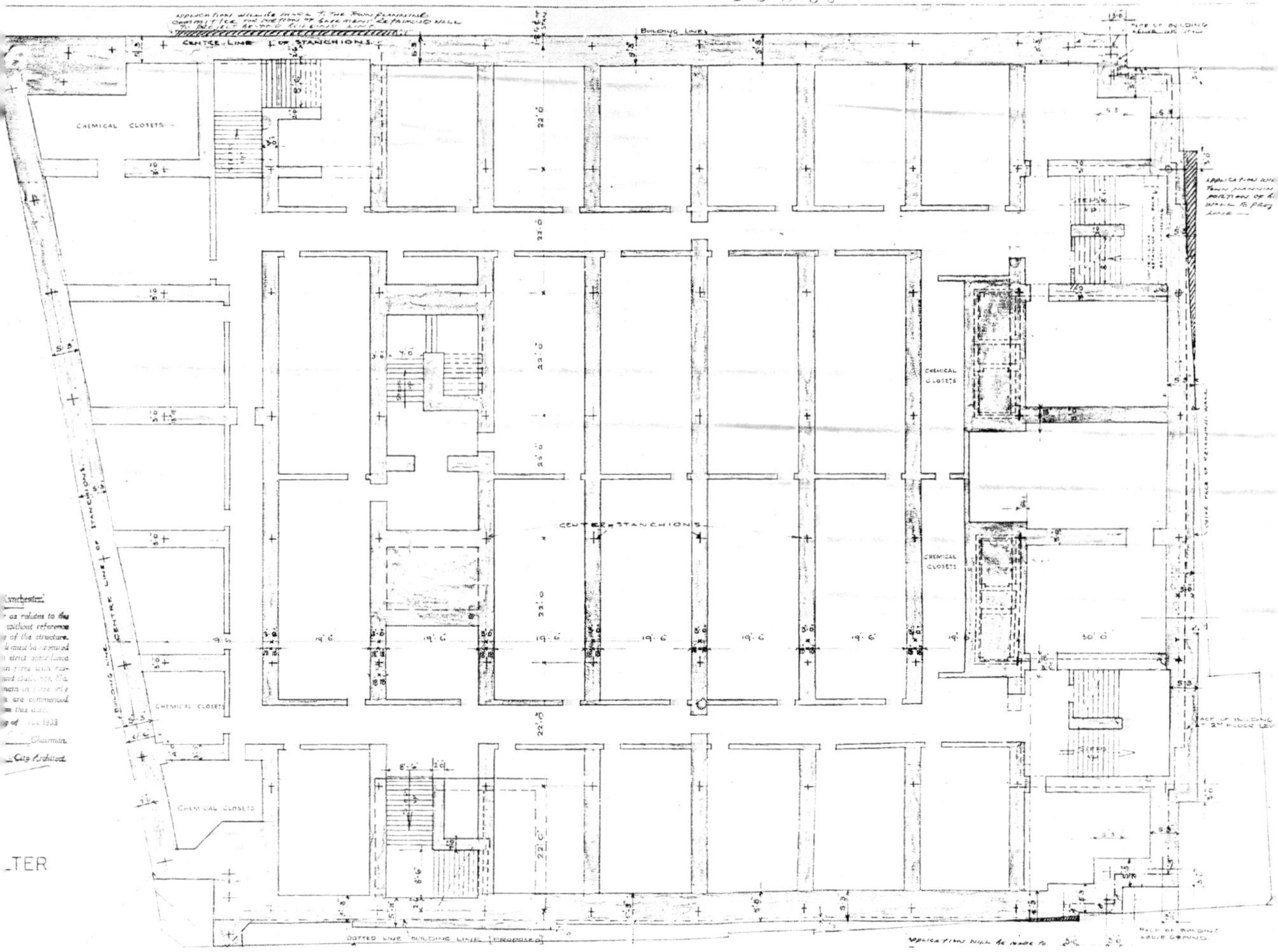

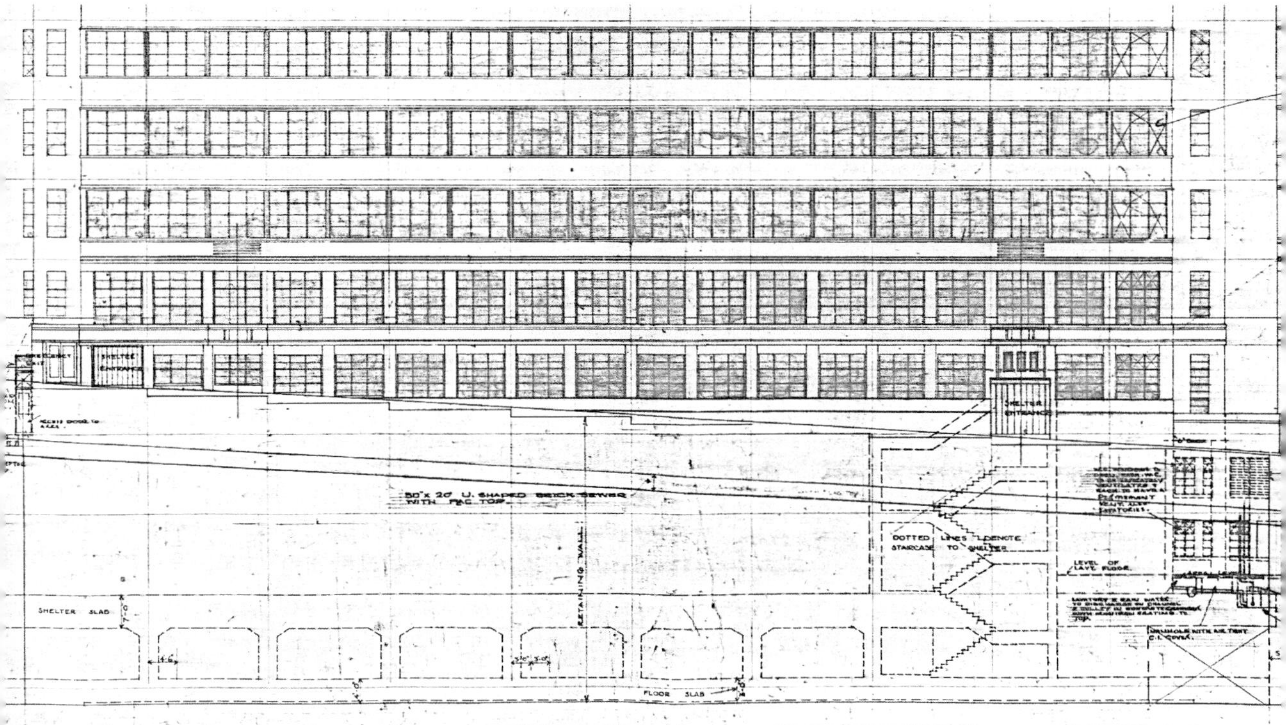

CENTRE LINE OF STANCHIONS

BUILDING LINES

LINE OF BUILDING

CHEMICAL CLOSETS

22'0

CENTRE LINE OF STANCHIONS

APPLICATION AND TOWN PLANNING PORTION OF BUILDING TO PROJECT

CHEMICAL CLOSETS

CENTRE OF STANCHIONS

CHEMICAL CLOSETS

19'6 19'6 19'6 19'6 50'0

CHEMICAL CLOSETS

22'0

CLOSET

CHEMICAL CLOSETS

DOTTED LINE BUILDING LINES (REMOVED)

APPLICATION WILL BE MADE TO

FACE OF BUILDING

_TER

ELEVATION   MAYES   STREET

SHELTER ENTRANCE

50'x 20' U SHAPED BRICK SEWER WITH REC. TOP.

DOTTED LINES DENOTE STAIRCASE TO SHELTER

LEVEL OF 1ST FLOOR

RETAINING WALL

SHELTER SLAB

FLOOR SLAB

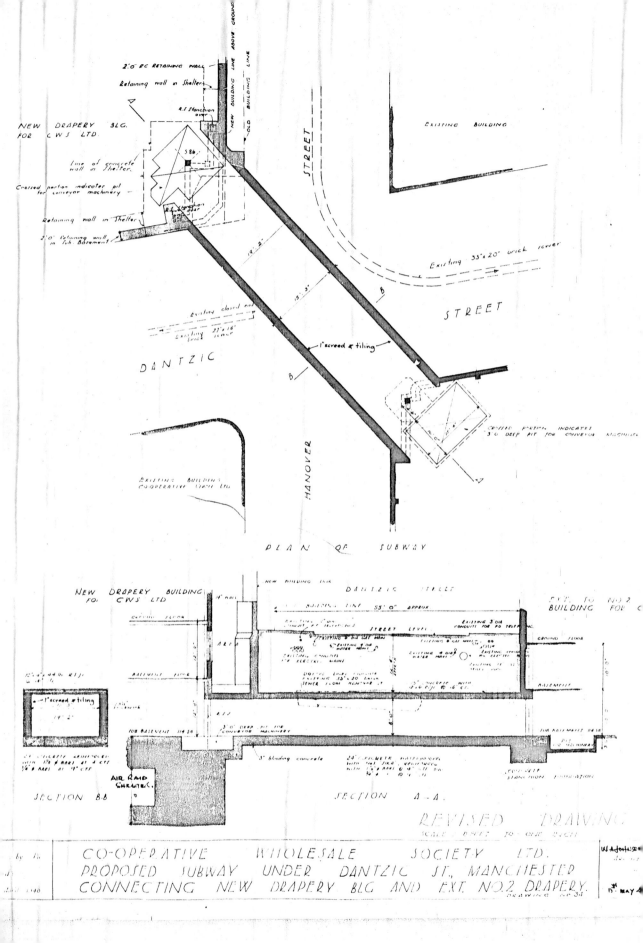

PLAN OF SUBWAY

SECTION B-B

AIR RAID SHELTER

SECTION A-A.

REVISED DRAWING

CO-OPERATIVE WHOLESALE SOCIETY LTD.
PROPOSED SUBWAY UNDER DANTZIC ST. MANCHESTER
CONNECTING NEW DRAPERY BLG AND EXT. NO.2 DRAPERY.

The building and the underground shelter were later the site for the CIS building. When work began in August 1959, a huge glacial boulder was unearthed. It was too big and hard to move or to break up and so it was buried below the 60ft level. Because this was the 'Cold War' era, the building had a fall-out shelter with the provision of enough air for three days' survival. Staircases down to the shelter areas remain today, and the four levels are used by the CIS for recreation facilities, staff restaurant, meetings and storage.

Opposite: Subway (6) under Dantzic Street

Below top: Stairs down to the fall-out shelters

Below bottom: Excavation on the CIS site

Below: CIS elevation with the WW2 shelter at the back

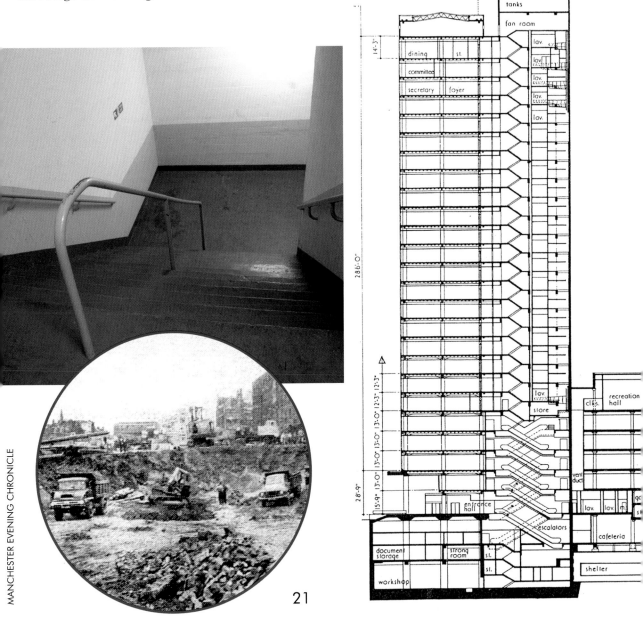

21

The old air raid shelter provided problems for the CIS builders, as the retaining wall had to be demolished by blasting. To reduce the risk of damage, the charges were covered with old tarpaulin and submarine nets. Some of the dimensions of the shelter were at slight variance with the war-time accounts. This time the walls of the shelter were said to be between 2ft and 4ft 6in and 35ft below. Five reinforced concrete staircase entrances into the shelter were demolished using pneumatic tools. In the lower levels below the CIS, there is evidence of blocked-off stairways which may be from the war-time shelter.

It is likely that the old subways will eventually be covered over, because the Co-op is planning to move to a new site. The future of the present buildings is uncertain, but it would seem possible they will be sold separately with no further requirement of the under-ground links. I am glad to have seen and recorded them before they disappear.

Above: Receptacle for bombs sent by post and sales room 1913
Below: CWS offices and warehouses 1912

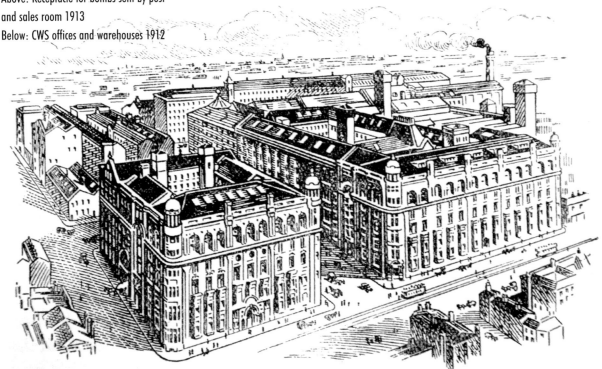

Above top: Refuge areas designated during the 'Cold War' period

Above: Tile design seen throughout the old Drapery building

Left: Remains of stairs under the CIS building, possibly when the site was used as a shelter

Victoria
Station

Left: The river Irk flows below the station, seen here from the old bridge. It was arched over, and the river bed paved in 1901, as part of the station extensions.

Below: The weir enhances the noise of the river as it rushes through the massive culvert.

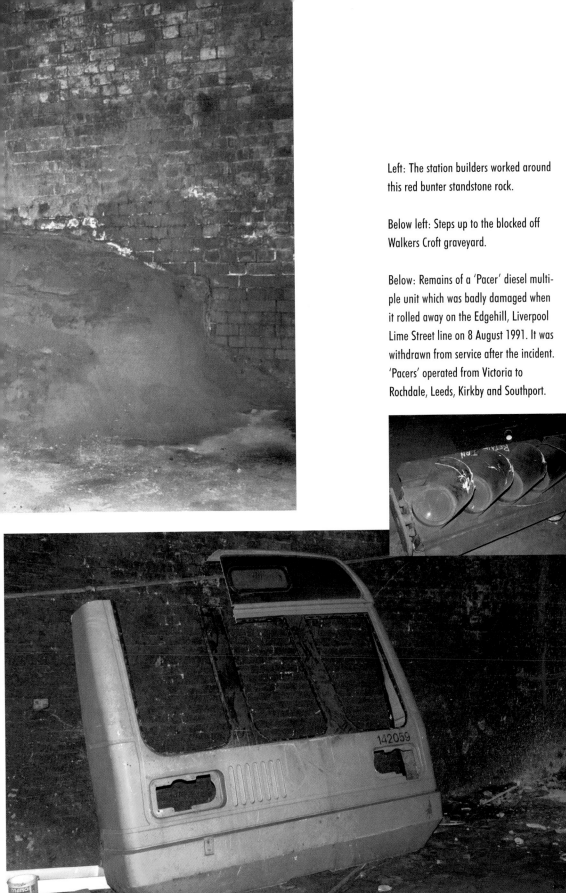

Left: The station builders worked around this red bunter standstone rock.

Below left: Steps up to the blocked off Walkers Croft graveyard.

Below: Remains of a 'Pacer' diesel multiple unit which was badly damaged when it rolled away on the Edgehill, Liverpool Lime Street line on 8 August 1991. It was withdrawn from service after the incident. 'Pacers' operated from Victoria to Rochdale, Leeds, Kirkby and Southport.

142059

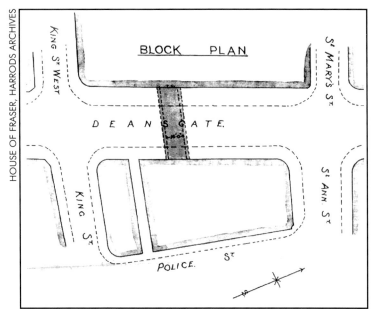

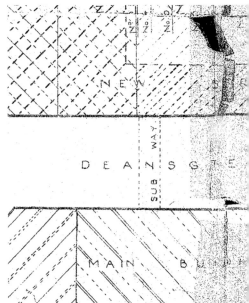

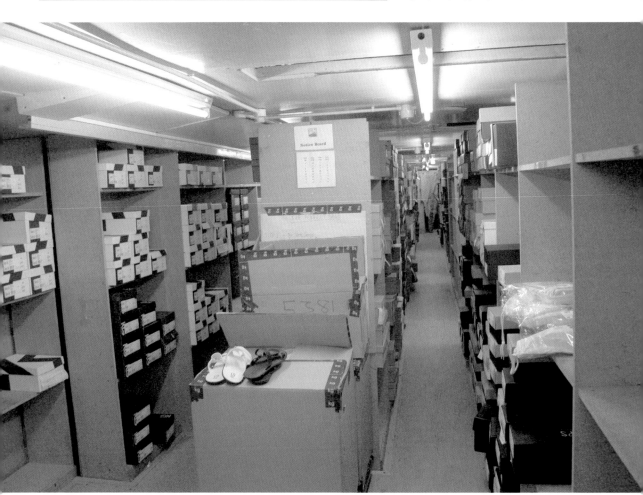

Kendal Milne

Plans from Kendals for a subway below Deansgate were submitted in December 1916, but not approved by Council in January 1917. Walter Herbert Milne, Frederick John Milne and Herbert Mowle Kendal were named as the first Licensees on this application.

Harrods bought Kendals in July 1919 for around £950,000, and amended plans were submitted on 23 July 1919 which showed the subway more at right angles across Deansgate, and the width increased from 13ft to 16ft. The subway was just above a corporation sewer which was 17ft 2in below street level.

The annual payment to Manchester Corporation was increased from the initial agreement of £250 to £300. The construction date was to be within six years.

The subway connected the main building on the east side with the growing acquisitions on the opposite side, known as the Star Buildings. The main building was extended to King Street West and opened on 17 November 1924.

A newspaper feature on the centenary of Kendals reported that the subway had opened in 1920, although the earliest referral to it in ads was 14 January 1921, when it was announced that the furnishing store in the main building could be accessed by 'the new subway under Deansgate'.

Opposite top left: Original 1916 plan for the subway set at an angle below Deansgate

Opposite top right: Later plan showing actual position of the subway

Below left and right: The once popular subway is currently used as storage space

KENDALS

re-open the

DEANSGATE SUBWAY

MONDAY NEXT, MAY 8

Kendals have great pleasure in announcing the re-opening of their Deansgate Subway. This will be of the greatest convenience to customers who wish to pass from the main building to the temporary Showrooms without having to negotiate the Deansgate traffic. The following Departments are located in the temporary showrooms of the new Kendals :

RADIOS, LAMPSHADES, LIBRARY, OCCASIONAL FURNITURE, TRUNKS, HARDWARE, ELECTRICAL, FURNISHING, DRAPERY, PIANOS, BOYS' WEAR, MEN'S WEAR, FURNITURE, DECORATION and CARPETS, REFRIGERATORS and PERAMBULATORS

Here are some typical examples of the special values which these Departments are offering :

GLASS

Special Offer of
ENGLISH CRYSTAL

GRAPE FRUIT GLASSES.
Special Price **2/-**

CUT CRYSTAL TANKARDS.
Pint size.   Special Price **4/-**

CUT CRYSTAL TANKARDS. **3/3**
Small.   Special Price

WATER JUGS.
Special Price **6/6**

SALAD BOWLS.
Special Price **10/9**

Special Price **7/6**

DECANTERS.
Special Price **14/9**

A new building, on the west side and completed in 1936 included basement space for 120 cars. By 1939, Kendals had three buildings on the west side of Deansgate and one on Southgate.

One of the west side buildings caught fire on 10 February 1939 and was one of the biggest blazes seen in the city for many years. The building covered half the site between King Street West and St Mary's Street with a frontage to Deansgate and had been due for demolition. The fire was first seen at the rear of the building at 8.20 pm and within fifteen minutes the whole building was engulfed in flames.

On the other half of the site, work was under way to construct a new seven-floor store for Kendals. The fire threatened the first phase of the new building up to St Mary's Street but the fire services managed to stop further damage. They flooded the Deansgate subway as a precaution to prevent the fire spreading to the main building on the east side of Deansgate. Just 200 yards along the road at the Deansgate Cinema, an audience, blissfully unaware of the events happening close by, were watching 'Too Hot to Handle'. Kendals opened at the usual time the following day, with the management promising that no-one would lose their jobs. The subway reopened on 8 May with a silverware display.

Preparations for war were at an advanced stage by April 1939, with the two lower floors of the new building excavated, and constructed with reinforced walls of concrete and steel which it was claimed would withstand a bomb blast in Deansgate. An advertisement announced that

KENDALS

CARRY ON ...

DURING air-raid alarms Kendals will carry on as usual until real danger threatens.

WHEN the 'Alert' sounds, shopping will continue in every department of the store and 'spotters' will at once take up their positions on roof-top breastworks to give further warning should danger seem imminent. Should this occur, everyone will be conducted to the Shelters by our own trained A.R.P. staff.

THE Shelters will, of course, be open for those who wish to go down on the first warning.

KENDALS Shelters in the sub-basement of the New Building are amongst the strongest and safest in the country, Above them is the enormously strong New Building with a ground floor of thick, reinforced concrete. A retaining wall of reinforced concrete all round the building gives added protection against concussion and blast.

Kendals have 16 Air-Raid Shelters 25 feet below ground

KENDAL MILNE & CO   ::   MANCHESTER 3

GUARDIAN

Shop in Safety at
KENDALS

16 AIR-RAID SHELTERS 25ft. BELOW GROUND

When the war began Kendals New Building in Deansgate was under construction, with deep excavations to sub-basement level already well advanced. It has been relatively easy, therefore, to build tremendously strong air-raid shelters in the sub-basement as an integral part of the building itself.

A thick retaining wall of reinforced concrete all round the building has been built to guard against blast and concussion. The dividing walls of the shelters are specially strengthened and reinforced. Above, two very thick, strong floors of reinforced concrete and the enormously strong steel frame of the new building give wonderful protection against all but a direct hit.

Altogether there are 16 shelter-rooms connected by doorways and corridors, and readily accessible from the Subway or from Southgate. One of them is illustrated above. There is comfortable accommodation for customers and staff—and should customers be detained below by an air-raid warning, tea or coffee would be served to those taking shelter.

With Christmas well on the way, it is good to know that shopping at Kendals is as safe as it is possible to make it. They're marvellous Shelters—but we trust we may never need to use them.

KENDAL MILNE & CO. ▪ DEANSGATE ▪ MANCHESTER, 3

there were 16 shelter rooms in the sub-basement. In 1939 a subway was also built under Southgate so that, in an emergency, people could be led from the buildings behind Deansgate to the new basement in comparative safety, 25ft underground. Work on the new subway was to be completed by early May of that year.

The third, fourth and fifth floors of the main store were requisitioned by the Government during the early years of the last war, and the top floor was used as a NAAFI.

The subway was closed off in 1981 and is now used for storage, but the Kendals' management have considered the possibility of opening it up again.

Above: The staff service subway under Southgate

Opposite: September 1939 advertisement

Below Boots

GUARDIAN

Top: Chamber ventilation

Above and overleaf: Work on the foundations of the Manchester Guardian building 1929

Opposite: Concrete bases in chambers below Boots

Steve Powell wrote to me about a deep-level space below the Boots site that he was shown at the time of the construction of the Arndale Centre around 1972. He remembered going down two flights of wooden steps to what looked like a storage area about 40 x 30 ft. Down a further two sets of stairs, his guide, a worker on the Arndale site, showed him a vast space that extended below Market Street and under the shopping centre. Steve recalled seeing old walls and bricks everywhere, and there was speculation that there was a GPO railway here. Today, it is difficult to know if that space is still there. I have explored the basements with Boots officials but they do not lead up Market Street. Possibly the areas seen in the 1970s have either been incorporated into the Arndale service areas or covered over when surplus to requirements. However, the Arndale management did show me a series of smaller chambers beneath Boots' basement. There were three parallel tunnels just over 40ft long. The two outer tunnels were over 6ft wide and high, while the middle chamber was over 11ft wide. Here were the remains of concrete bases - possibly for printing machinery or other associated processes, for the Manchester Guardian and Evening News. The brickwork in the chambers looks comparatively recent and could be connected with the building of the Arndale Centre. Deep-level work began on new offices and printing facilities for the Manchester Guardian in 1929, and this chamber may be an extension to it.

My father was the manager of the Saxone shoe shop on Market Street, Manchester and I used to work there as a 'Saturday' job (started on 10 shillings a day!) when I was in my early teens, a long time ago in the 50s. I do recall the old 'service' lift (not for customer use) went down to a sub-basement below the basement and opened out into a largely disused area with the only lighting being by the lift gate, just some old rubbish (perhaps bits of shop fittings) being down there. The space then went away into the darkness. My father did tell me that it was part of 'underground' Manchester and I recall him saying that you could go as far as the Old Sam's Chop House, but of course I do not know if this is true. If the 'tunnel' exists then it is possibly below Market Street or the shops opposite the Arndale, but my memory is from long ago.

IAN WHYTE

Underground miscellany

Post Office Railway mystery

I am often asked about an underground railway which is said to have been operated by the Post Office. So far I have these accounts:

Cliff Brierley's father, who worked in the Manchester sewers, told him that there was an old underground Post Office railway in the 1950s. There was an entrance to it at Piccadilly Station via a lift near platforms 13 and 14. He thought the route was circular, calling at Victoria and Central. His father claimed he had seen a small electric engine about 4ft long, 100ft underground.

There was a Post Office underground transportation system which ran from All Saints Post office to the PO in the centre of the city. It was not big enough to allow anyone to travel on it. It was some form of electric traction, and I think it finally stopped working c1950 to 1954. My Dad, who was a Superintendent (Postal), referred to it frequently during my younger years.

DONALD HENDERSON

I have also been told it was built during the last war from York Street Post Office and was intended to link up with the main post office in Spring Gardens. It was intended for parcel traffic, but was never completed.

● *I should like to hear from anyone who may know more about this railway.*

Shaft of unknown origin under a warehouse at the Museum of Science and Industry

DEANSGATE TUNNEL

In January 1905, a representative of the Waterman's Association wrote to the Guardian newspaper about the dangers of the Deansgate tunnel on Whitworth Street. He described how steam and fog combined to make visibility impossible. People and horses had veered off the towpath into the canal as they became disorientated. The writer suggested the tunnel should be lit and that a handrail be placed either by the side of the canal or on the tunnel wall.

Waterwheel chamber below the Piccadilly Basin car park, photographed in 1989.

The photo (left) shows the 80ft shaft. The end has been blocked by a roof fall during demolition of the mill which was above it.

38

The Heaton Park Tunnel Mystery

On 12 February 1883 railway workers in the tunnel near Heaton Park heard groaning in the darkness and found, lying between the outer rail and the tunnel wall, a man with cuts and bruising to his face and head.

He seemed confused and agitated, and his only concern was that he had lost his hat. The workers managed to hold the man down while another train passed through the tunnel and then took him to Prestwich Hospital. He was examined and his injuries treated and then later released.

Grim discovery

The railway workers went back to the tunnel to look for the man's lost hat. It was then they made a grim discovery. About 300 yards further along the line from where they had found the man, they came across a badly injured woman. Her legs had been severed and she was taken to the Infirmary but died soon afterwards.

It was assumed that both had been passengers on the 2.40pm train from Manchester to Radcliffe, but how did they end up on the line inside the tunnel? There was no evidence of a struggle in the train carriage where umbrellas and the man's overcoat were found.

Identified

The pair were later identified as Mr and Mrs Kay from Radcliffe. James was a wealthy retired merchant, and he and his wife Harriet had travelled to Manchester to deposit money at a bank as well as conducting other business. After further enquiries, James was to be charged with the death of his wife.

His only explanation of the events in the tunnel was that 'he had got out of the carriage to see a boy of his who was at school.' Medical evidence showed that James was mentally unstable and had suicidal tendencies. However without witnesses it was not possible to be sure whether James had tried to kill himself or had deliberately pushed his wife out of the carriage.

The magistrate decided that because of the lack of evidence and the man's state of mind, he should be discharged and be placed by his family and friends in secure care for the rest of his life.

Underground to Piccadilly

While working on a building in the vicinity of London Road and Fairfield Street in 1972, an employee came across a tunnel leading to Piccadilly. It was an electricity duct and he was told it led to the old Woolworth's and Paulden's stores. The passage was around 6ft 6ins high and six ft wide. It was a straight route, and seemed to run parallel with London Road, presumably going below the old fire station. Lights automatically went on and off as he went through sections of the duct which had steel double doors. He could hear the sound of rats, and as he was in his dinner hour he decided to turn back and did not get as far as Piccadilly.

Huge 19th century drainage shaft 20 ft below ground in premises on Minshull Street

Tunnel fire under Oxford Street

A fire broke out in a cable tunnel running up Oxford Street towards the Midland Hotel on the 17 January 1930. The tunnel, 4ft 6in high and 13ft below the street, was being excavated by candle light when, at around nine o'clock in the evening, workers unexpectedly uncovered a leaking gas pipe. There was a sudden flash of light and an explosion and the seven workmen quickly made for the exit outside the hotel. Robert Pooley, the foreman, bore the brunt of the blast and he was pulled out dazed and suffering from slight gas poisoning.

The timber supports had caught fire and there were flames coming from the gas pipe. Crowds gathered to watch as the Fire Brigade hosed the tunnel, which still emitted clouds of steam and smoke. It was thought that the situation was under control but at eleven o'clock a fire broke out in another part of the tunnel and flames leapt above the road. More excavations began, to trace the source of the leak which had produced a strong smell of gas around Oxford Street. At 12.30 a further explosion was heard as the excavation work continued, and more flames and smoke poured out.

Just after 2am workmen discovered the source of the problem, a perforated 6in gas main crossing the roof of the tunnel. They tried to make a temporary repair by covering it with a large plaster but had to get out quickly before they were overcome by gas. Finally a fire brigade official went down and secured the plaster with rope.

Barton Arcade

One of the old gates which used to lift up to close off the Barton Arcade on Deansgate, is now in the permanent down position in the basement

PRINTWORKS TUNNEL

Bob Magee, formerly Chief Engineer at Thomson Newspapers, had heard of the claims but had never seen a tunnel below the site - said to run from the River Irwell, up to Smithfield Market and on to Piccadilly. There were cable ducts at low level.

Possible covered-over tunnel on the Print Works site

Another former employee recalled the exposed brick culvert, visible on a photo, but did not know what lay beyond the entrance. The base of the site covered over cellars. There was an egg-shaped sewer below, and a concrete slab running the length of the site, thought to be part of the printing hall.

Arches and culverts under Marshall Street

The Lancastrian School was built in 1812 on Marshall Street between Rochdale Road and Oldham Road. It was later handed to the Manchester School Board and during rebuilding in 1907, workmen discovered two old arches in the foundations. One arch was 17ft across and 10ft high. The other, smaller arch extended 10ft under the road. It was thought the site was previously a work-place with rumours of wells. During excavations in the cellar, longer culverts were found with sealed ends at the building boundaries.

King Street and St Ann's Square

William Ponter wrote in the City News in 1925 how he had once walked beneath King Street to St Ann's Square. Mr Ponter had already attracted much public attention in 1903 with the discovery of a magnificent crypt beneath his own furniture showroom on Old Millgate. People marvelled at this architectural curiosity 30ft below pavement level.

The journey began one Sunday morning in the cellar of Taylor's haberdashery shop, King Street. He went with the owner Richard Bramwell Taylor, well known in the city for his work with underprivileged children in founding the Ragged Schools. They took along two dogs because they expected rats. The far cellar under the shop had an opening which brought them under King Street, and then onto the shops at St Ann's Place. They were actually walking through cellars and it brought them as far as the well-stocked wine cellar at the corner of St Ann's Square, thought to be the premises of Frank Drury Ltd. The same route was tried again the next day but the entrance to the wine cellars had been blocked off.

I enquired at the premises on King Street, and found that, during a refit of the shop some time ago, a passage under the stairs had been uncovered and a way below

Opposite above: King Street today - once an underground walkway

Opposite below: St Ann's Passage

43

King Street had been found. It would not have been possible to go as far as Mr Ponter and Mr Taylor had because of a newer building on the corner.

This underground route reminded me of the apparent discovery of a crypt close to St Ann's Church, under St Ann's Passage. An article in St Ann's Church's monthly magazine in December 1930, gave a description of the vaulted arches below the premises of Marshall and Snelgrove. It was presumed that there would be a connection between the vaults and the church, and there was speculation that the church would raise money to carry out further excavation and plan to use it as a

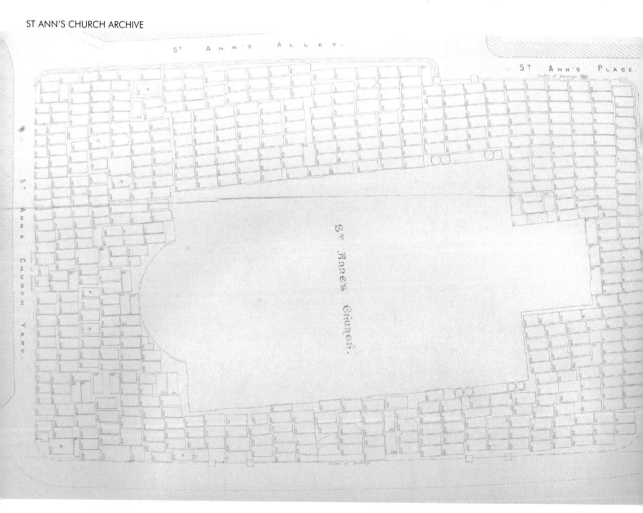

chapel. The existence of this underground ecclesiastical space came as a surprise as there were no plans or other documents which referred to it. The idea was raised again in the church's magazine in April 1937 and the Rector was thinking about how the crypt could be used. It would provide space for a vestry, a chapel for special services, or a place of contemplation.

There has been no mention of the crypt since. Today, it seems to have been completely forgotten. When I mentioned it to the present Verger, Paul, he knew nothing of it, and neither did any of the older parishioners he talked to. I also contacted the previous advisory architect to the church and he was also mystified. Could there have been a crypt here or was there another explanation? I had also heard rumours of an underground

Above: The 'crypt' found in 1930

Opposite: St Ann's grave plan with no indication of vaults under St Ann's passage

Above: Cellaring discovered below King Street, dating back to the late 17th or early 18th century, from a previous building. Similar cellars had been found in Old Millgate, St Mary's Gate and Deansgate. They were thought to be used for storing wine and beer

passage from Habitat. Staff at the store on St Ann's Street were convinced that a route led from there beneath the street towards the church. Some had seen the entrance to the passage but had not ventured into it for safety reasons. The route would have led under St Ann's passage, so were we about to make an exciting discovery? In the spring of 2008 I went to find the tunnel with a small group of Habitat employees, along with James who had first told me about it. To our great disappointment, despite a good look in the maze of cellars, the original entrance could not be found. Refurbishment work had been carried out in the cellars and we did come to dead ends closed off with breeze blocks - were they covering an entrance?

I later talked to Roger Fitzgerald who once managed the

flower stall by St Ann's Church. He had taken a keen interest in the history of the area but had not heard of a tunnel below St Ann's Passage. However he did point out two significant things. He said that the edge of the present shoe shop canopy was the boundary of the old Marshall & Snelgrove store. The 'crypt' therefore, that had been discovered in the basement, was within the boundaries of the previous store rather than beneath the present passage. Also, as he ran his stall, he kept a close watch on the deep excavations being dug just a few feet away on St Ann's Street, which had not revealed any tunnels between the Habitat building and the church.

So, if there was no route below the road, what was the explanation for the spaces under Habitat and the Marshall & Snelgrove building? In the past, arching under here had been interpreted as blocked up entrances, but it was just a device often used by builders on end walls to economise on bricks. Therefore what seemed to be a route leading towards the church, in the absence of any other evidence, was more likely to have been an area of storage and possibly an employees' air raid shelter.

Now that I knew the original boundaries to Marshall Snelgrove's, I looked again at the insurance plans of the area and found the location of the crypt was previously old vaulted wine cellars. There would have been no link with the church, and the vault did not extend into the old boundaries of St Ann's Passage. So the wine cellars were those visited by Mr Ponter and Mr Taylor around 1880, and are the so-called 'lost crypt'. Perhaps the people at St Ann's Church after examining the facts, realized many years ago that they were not going to find a crypt and quietly dropped their claims.

Change of paving, indicating the old building boundary

The Manchester Arms

Terry Hull was an apprentice joiner in about 1961. He went below the jewellers next to the Rovers Return (then a cafe) on Shudehill which was closed for renovation. There was light in the cellar coming from the glass tiles in the street above, and the walls were whitewashed. They knocked out bricks with a chisel and found a hole. Further inspection revealed the top of an arch. He could not recall in which direction the tunnel went. He and a work-mate shone a torch in - it was damp, they could hear water dripping and rats squealing. Unsurprisingly they didn't venture further.

Ken Wilson remembered the tunnels beneath the Manchester Arms in the 1960s. He lived there with his father who was the landlord, when there were three other pubs in the vicinity. One tunnel went back towards Corporation Street, another went towards Victoria Station, and a third to Chethams. The entrances were bricked up to half the height so that he had to climb over. The tunnels were old and filthy and built of brick.

A tunnel went towards the Fish Dock at Victoria Station. It was damp, big enough to stand in, and wide, with brick arching. A drier tunnel went up a rising slope to Shudehill (See account left). Ken recalled a bus station in the road, and that there were coffins lying against the windows outside a shop. He could see them from below through a steel grille. The brick steps out of the tunnel were near the Fish Market on Shudehill.

The tunnel to Chethams and the Cathedral was damp, and it went under the school at Chethams. He also remembered when he could walk through the Victoria Arches via steps at Hunts Bank. The door of the British Rail Social Club, which led into the tunnels, was always open. The club was full of people from the newspaper works who would drink there throughout the day.

Gaskell's Baths

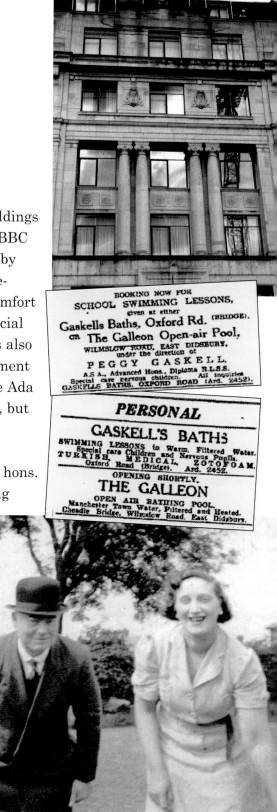

Gaskell's pool was underground in the Imperial Buildings by the Oxford Road bridge, and next to the present BBC studios. The pool was privately owned and just 20ft by 8ft, and 4ft deep. It opened on 21 July 1930 with life-saving classes and swimming lessons in 'warmth, comfort and privacy' given by Mrs Ada Frances Gaskell. Special attention was given to nervous pupils and there was also an electro-turkish bath, sunray, massage, and treatment for obesity and rheumatism. Census records indicate Ada had been a library assistant before she was married, but her sister, Harriet, was a swimming teacher.

In May 1934, Ada's daughter Peggy, (ASA advanced hons. diploma RLSS), took over the private daily swimming lessons in the 'pure filtered water'. Additional facilities offered were Zotafoam baths, hairdressing salon and chiropody.

In January 1937, 'Peggy' (Kathleen Margaret) married Albert Bradley of Withington and later that year they opened the Galleon open-air swimming pool at Cheadle Bridge, East Didsbury. Peggy continued to give swimming lessons at both venues until Gaskell's closed in 1963. She featured in a 'Guardian' article in 1959, with a description of the sauna at Gaskell's, which she claimed was the only one in the country outside London.

Peggy and Albert Bradley at the Galleon

49

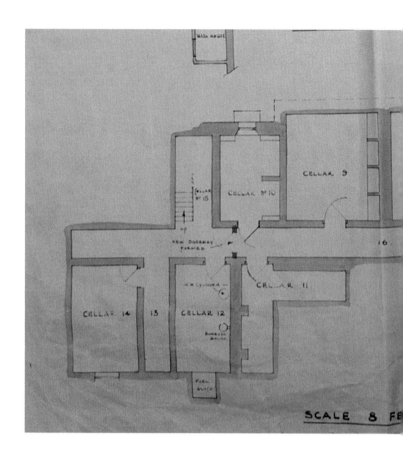

As a Boy Scout, our Saturday meetings were held in one of the attics at the Horsfall Museum. I clearly remember one rainy afternoon the museum guide (a kind man and ex-Scout) asked us if we would care to see the dungeons. Would we! I was 12 years old and believed all an adult in authority told me.
He took us down into the cellars (after locking the doors to the public) and down further steep steps to sub-cellars. Here was a long passage going in several directions with rooms let into the sides. These he told us were cells to hold prisoners in chains. He led us some short way along and said we were under Every Street and the Round House. Here there was rubble piled to stop our way.

He explained there were passages going along Pin Mill Brow to Ardwick and under Ancoats Lane to Manchester Cathedral. His reason for these passages was that the wealthy people lived in difficult changing times and sometimes required an escape from either their home or church from the authorities.

RON TRULIO

Ancoats Hall

Anthony Middleton was born 1943. From the age of six he lived in Ardwick until he was nine. His father, who was a steel worker at English Steel in Clayton, took him to see the Horsfall Museum at Ancoats in 1949. The museum had closed for the night but the heating was still on. They were taken on a tour by the night-watchman who was a friend of his father.

The main reason was to see the 'Oliver Cromwell tunnel'. Anthony is not sure where he accessed the tunnel - at ground level or cellar - but there was a large wooden door set into the floor, about 6ft square. It was raised by a chain over a block and tackle.

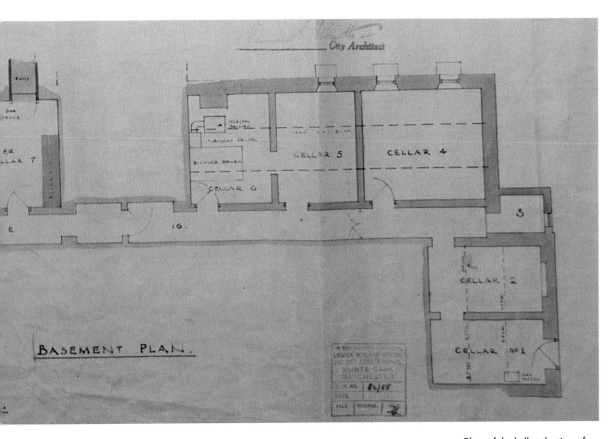

CELLAR 5

CELLAR 4

ER
LLAR 7

CELLAR 6

IO.

CELLAR 2

BASEMENT PLAN.

CELLAR N°1

Plans of the hall at the time of
its ownership by British Rail as a
social club in 1955. It is not clear
if it is the basement passage being
referred to on these pages, or
whether there is a deeper route.

Below was an enormous staircase - as you would see in
a tube station. It was about 6ft wide and the tunnel below
was electrically lit. It had an earth floor with sandstone
walls. It was about 7-8ft high and wide enough for four
horses to have walked along. This was the spot where
the horses were fed and watered. There was a large stone
trough opposite the staircase.

He saw four openings leading away from the main
tunnel. He could see around 150ft into the distance.
It was bricked off at the end, although there appeared
to be many escape passages about 2ft wide.

The watchman claimed the tunnel went to Clayton and
the Cathedral, where there was a network below the city
centre. The tunnel was in darkness in the other direction,
but it felt dry.

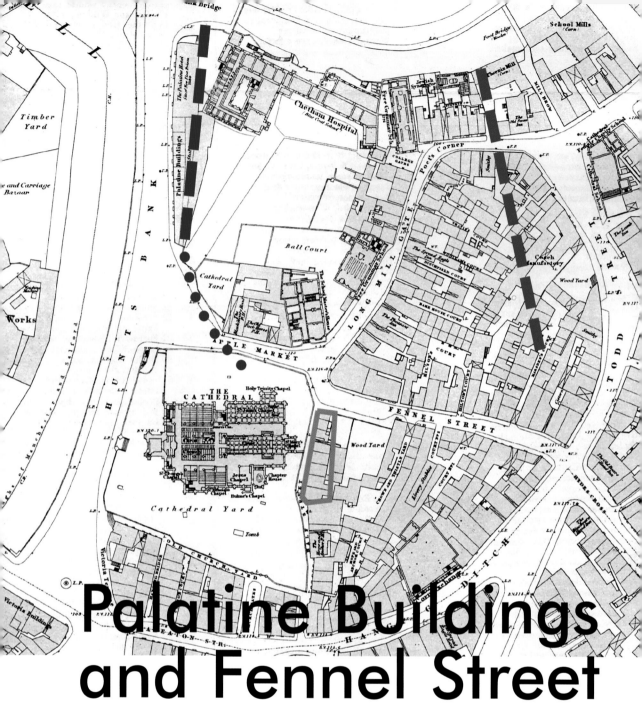

Palatine Buildings and Fennel Street

1849 map with the possible routes of the underground trench from the Cathedral to the river, and the drainage tunnel to the Irk. Also shown are the premises with vaulted cellars and passages

Opposite: Palatine Hotel completed 1843 and Palatine Buildings

During construction of the Palatine Hotel at Hunts Bank, workmen uncovered a trench cut into the rock, around 12ft down. A vertical cross-section resembled the shape of an inverted church bell, measuring around 13ft at the top and 2ft at the bottom. The trench ran parallel with Hunts Bank from the north end of the buildings to the River Irk. It was arched where it passed beneath the inclined road to Victoria Station. Another portion of the trench was discovered during work on the Palatine Buildings which adjoined the hotel. This led to speculation that this was the route of an old watercourse from the college or the collegiate church. Full-size human bones were discovered at the upper end of the trench but it was not known how they got there.

A 1827 newspaper advertisement for the sale of property bounded by Fennel Street and Todd Street included a tunnel. Along with stables, smithies, warehouses, and cottages and a well, the premises also had their own drainage tunnel, described as 'spacious', going down to the River Irk. The site would have been beneath the present Cathedral Gardens by Urbis.

A writer to the Guardian in 1937 dismissed reports of bodies with stakes through them, in old premises on the east side of the Cathedral. He was present when the new buildings were being erected and the excavations went down to virgin ground. No tunnels were found but there were vaulted cellars and passages which belonged to the old premises. Vaulting was a regular mode of construction in basements of older buildings, and had also been seen during demolition of buildings at the corner of Millgate, Hanging Ditch and Cannon Street.

Above: The riverside rocks and caves

Right: Map by Charles Roeder, 1900

Below: The site of the Irwell caves today

River caves

In May 1899, four caves were examined by local historian, Charles Roeder (1848-1911), cut into the rock by the edge of the River Irwell at the Parsonage, close to Blackfriars Bridge. They were filled with mud, and measured 4ft deep, up to 6ft high, and just over 3ft wide. Another cave was discovered by the River Irk at Old Millgate, during demolition of houses on the river bank in preparation for the extension to Victoria Station. The cave was 12ft high, around 8ft wide and a substantial depth.

Higher up the river, near Hargreaves Street, two caves or chambers had been previously discovered, around 10ft high and had been explored to a distance of 30ft. The pick marks of the builders could be seen. By the late 1800s they were used for the disposal of sewage. The discovery of coins, pottery and other artifacts in and around the Irk and Irwell suggests that all the caves could have been ancient shelters and refuges.

Rusholme Road Cemetery

The old Non-Conformist cemetery opened around 1821 and 8,596 people were buried there. It was a privately-funded graveyard - the first of its kind in the country. Most of the cemetery was paved with flat gravestones. Many eminent people were interred here including John Edward Taylor, the founder of the Manchester Guardian; Sophia Russell Scott, first wife of John Ryland; and 'the ebony phenomenon' boxer James Robinson who died of cholera in 1849. Burials continued until 1933, but by the 1940s the cemetery was in poor condition and coffins had been broken into. Vandals also got into the cellars of the ruined lodge which had been damaged by a bomb during the Blitz.

There was a tunnel linking the vaults in the south western corner of the cemetery. A newspaper reporter, in 1947, described the tunnel as 'black and airless' and walked only twelve paces along it, with the help of the light from matches, before turning back. In 1954 the cemetery came into the ownership of Manchester Corporation and the site of the cemetery is now covered by Gartside Gardens and a playground close to Upper Brook Street.

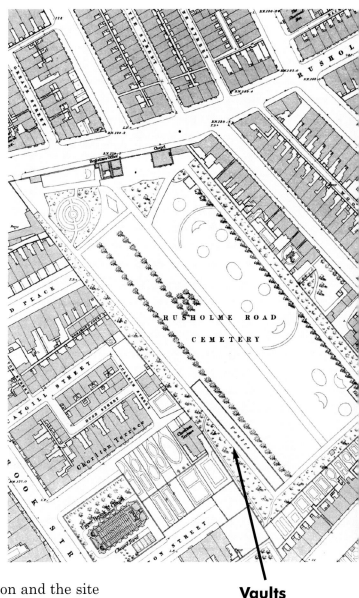

Vaults

55

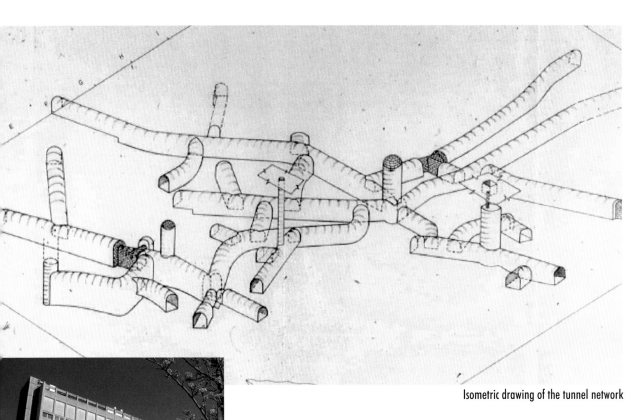

Isometric drawing of the tunnel network

UMIST

A tunnel network was discovered during a site investigation of 'Area B' UMIST in January 1968. It was thought to have been used as a storage area for the Garratt Print Works above, and then later to dispose of waste from a nearby works. A preliminary inspection was carried out in April, and then in March 1969 K Wardell and Partners were commissioned to provide a survey to find out the extent and condition of the tunnels in order to infill them. A 36in diameter access shaft was opened, and a series of probes made. The tunnels were generally sound, but a pump had to be used continuously to keep the water down to a reasonable level. 350m of tunnels and seven shafts were found during the survey.

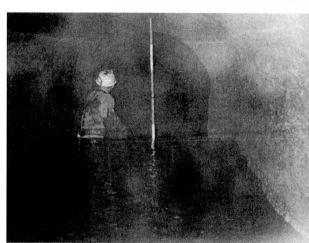

1849 map showing the print works
above the water storage tunnels

Opposite: The UMIST tunnel network
which linked to the river Medlock

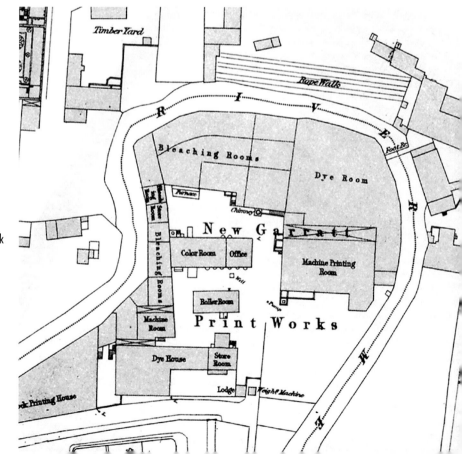

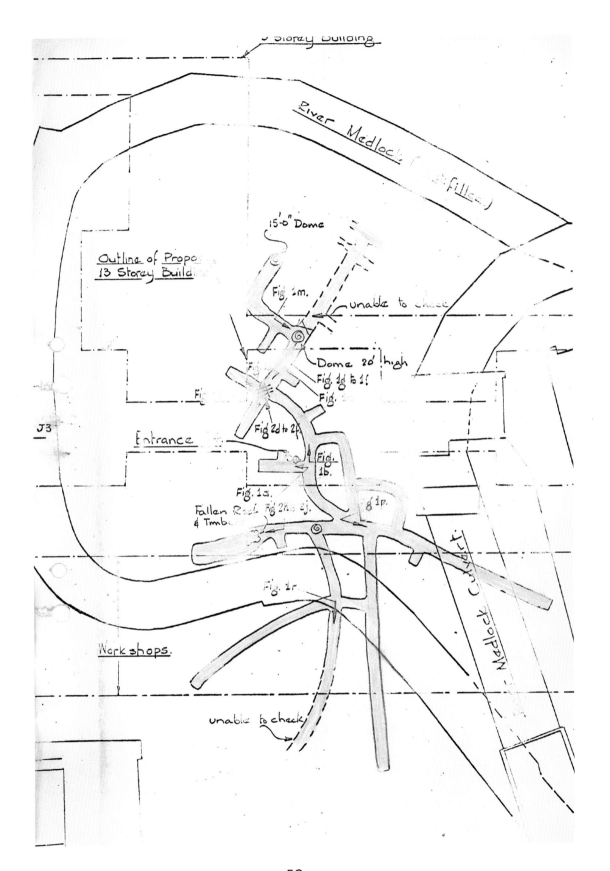

River Medlock (part filled)

3 Storey Building

15'-0" Dome

Outline of Propo[...]
13 Storey Build[...]

Fig. 2m.

unable to check

Dome 20' high
Fig. 1g to 1[...]
Fig. [...]

Fi[...]

Fig. [...]

J3

Fig 2d to 2[...]

Entrance

Fig.
1b.

Fig. 1a.

Fallen Roof Fig 2k [...]
& Timb[...]

Fig 1p.

Fig. 1r.

Workshops.

Medlock Culvert.

unable to check

59

The people of Manchester spent substantial time below ground as they took refuge from enemy bombing raids during the last world war.

The authorities had not envisaged people having to stay for such long periods in shelters, and had only provided the most basic of facilities. When the bombing began, it soon became clear that the communal shelters were inadequate. Many were wet and cold, and lacking in toilets and medical facilities. They were often poorly lit and were not kept clean. Drunkenness, lack of parental control and vandalism also caused problems. Supervision of shelters had not been organised and there was no provision of shelter marshals

There was initial uncertainty between local and national government as to who had responsibility to rectify these problems.  This chapter highlights the gradual improvement of conditions in those difficult days of war. Letters, announcements and advertisements illustrate the thoughts, the pressures and problems of the public and the authorities. As we look at life in the underground shelter, we may be both amazed and saddened by the conditions which that generation had to endure.

Here also is a list of the official public underground shelters in the City, as well as details of the network of below-ground control centres which monitored and responded to enemy action and damage.

Control rooms

THE POLICE

In 1939 provision had been made for under-ground Police report and control centres with telephone links in each of the divisions.

Central Control
Police headquarters, South Street,
off Albert Square

A Division
The City Police Courts, Minshull Street

B Division
1. Willert Street Police Station (Miles Platting)
2. Park House, Crumpsall

Opposite above and below: Thought
to be the Dickenson Road control centre

Below: Central Control

GUARDIAN

C Division

1. Mill Street Police Station, Bradford
2. Cellars in the former Croft Street Mills, Gorton

D Division

Moss Side Library

Rusholme Library, Dickenson Road

(Platt Lane Police Station was not used because it did not have a basement). The library was rented at £40 per annum excluding costs for heating, lighting and cleaning.

MANCHESTER LIBRARIES

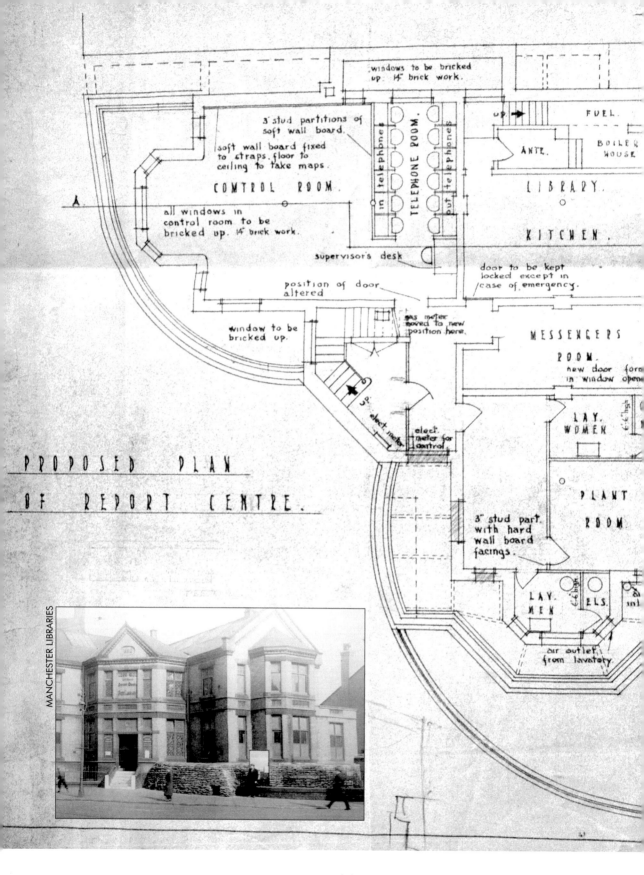

windows to be bricked
up. 14" brick work.

up. FUEL.

3" stud partitions of
soft wall board.

ANTE. BOILER
HOUSE

soft wall board fixed
to straps, floor to
ceiling to take maps.

LIBRARY.

CONTROL ROOM.

all windows in
control room to be
bricked up. 14" brick work.

KITCHEN.

in telephones

TELEPHONE ROOM.

put telephones

supervisor's desk

door to be kept
locked except in
case of emergency.

position of door
altered

gas meter
moved to new
position here.

window to be
bricked up.

up

elect. meter

elect.
meter for
control

MESSENGERS
ROOM.

new door form
in window open

LAV.
WOMEN

PROPOSED PLAN
OF REPORT CENTRE.

PLANT
ROOM

3" stud part.
with hard
wall board
facings.

LAV.
MEN

ELS.

air outlet
from lavatory.

MANCHESTER PUBLIC LIBRARIES

ADMINISTRATION DEPARTMENT

CHARLES NOWELL, M.A. F.L.A.
CHIEF LIBRARIAN

Telephone: Central 1992

**CENTRAL LIBRARY
ST. PETER'S SQUARE
MANCHESTER. 2**

11th August 19 41

MEMORANDUM TO the Chief Librarian

Mr. Cole of Moss Side reports that Superintendent Smith of Platt Lane Police Station visited him and said that the Police are to picket the Control Centre and visit it every hour, day and night. There is to be an armed constable on duty outside the building 24 hours a day, who will be responsible for the Control Centre, Fire Station and Police Station. The Police desire authority to patrol the library at any time. No fire watchers will be needed. *(Smith says he never said this)*

The Home Guard, who were to have placed a guard over the Control Centre, have not done so since last November, so the police now intend to take it over.

brick w

N.B. all windows except the control room to be sand-bagged.

pavement level.

Moss Side Control Centre
Situated in Moss Side Library on Denmark Road, now covered by the brewery site

Above: Memo regarding the change of security for the Centre

Left: Plan showing the Control Room layout

Left inset: The heavily sandbagged library building

Below: The escape route

stair to be opened up for access to boiler house and escape from centre.

STAFF CLOAK ROOM.

new stair formed of pre-cast concrete. 7" rise & 9" tread.

concrete lintle

4½" brick work

Window to be broken out for 3'-6" x 7'-0" door formed.

SECTION THRO B-B.

THE COUNCIL

Another control centre in Manchester Town Hall basement co-ordinated civic services from the districts. There were 14 District depots from which first aid, decontamination and rescue and demolition services operated.

Barbara Shaw was too young for the forces so she joined the Civil Defence. She was in the medical service centre (Manchester Health Department) in the basement of the Town Hall which manned a 24 hour service with three teams. Each team worked a week.

She was a telephonist for the hospital, first aid posts and mortuaries. Barbara slept with six other girls in a dormitory in the Town Hall where there was a huge yellow air raid warning bell. When it sounded they all rushed to the control centre.

By 1940 at 17 years old, she was the youngest Civil Defence worker, and at Christmas she was kept busy with the Blitz which lasted two nights. She could hear the rumblings of the incendiary bombs on the Town Hall but they were quickly put out. St Peter's Square was ringed by fallen buildings. The bombing in Princess Street was dreadful. The team were underneath in the electricity showroom's basement. Later in the war they were transferred to the old Town Hall on the side nearest St Peter's Square.

She controlled the movements of the ambulances. There was a huge map which indicated where bombs had fallen. From the control room they directed where rescuers should go.

Underground tunnels were used as shelters, and she remembers going to one of them where people huddled in their bedding. She went in a lift to the top of the Ritz and could see the city ablaze. At the time she lived on Heyes Lane, Timperley, and went into Manchester by electric train, working one week in three from Sunday to Sunday starting at 5.30pm.

CONTROL

No admittance except for control staffs

EMERGENCY DOOR

TOOLS TO BREAK THROUGH
THE THIN STONEWORK WILL
BE FOUND IN THE EMERGENCY
TOOL STORE.

NORTH WEST REGIONAL CONTROL ROOM

The War Room was situated at the Headquarters of the north west region Civil Defence in the basement of Arkwright House, in Parsonage Gardens. 'Region 10', the area of control, stretched from the Scottish border down

to south Cheshire under the first Regional Commissioner, Sir Warren Fisher. Britain was split into twelve areas to organise civil defence. In the event of an invasion with a region being cut off from central government, Regional Commissioners were granted powers under the Defence of the Realm Regulations known as 'DORA'. Under the King's Warrant the Regional Commissioner held power of government over the seven and a half million people in Lancashire, Cheshire, Cumberland, Westmorland and the High Peak of Derbyshire. The Commissioner would hold full powers and issue orders to the area Army Commander. Arkwright House had been briefly used from 1937 to train police and

fire brigade personnel in anti-gas methods. The building, by the architect Harry S Fairhurst, had been constructed for the headquarters of the English Sewing Cotton Company in 1927.

Top: Sir Warren Fisher

Left: The arrival of Sir Warren Fisher (left) at London Road Station, being met by his staff - Major VR Kenny (centre) and Major Broadhurst (right)

Details about the War Room are obtained from a series of newspaper articles designed to encourage and reassure the public during the war, so it is not clear how accurate they are and how much misinformation they contain. However, much of the detail can be confirmed in the photographs alongside the articles and by some of the surviving features of the war-time Control Room below Manchester Town Hall, as well as other documents.

The specially-protected War Room, where sixty people worked eight-hour shifts, was entered down steps, then through a heavily reinforced corridor with shelters for the staff on either side. The walls were painted light and dark green and the pipes stood out in red. There was a small wooden gate with a 'private' notice on it leading to a large set of steel airlock doors which guarded the top-secret War Room. One report states that the entrance was guarded by soldiers with fixed bayonets.

MANCHESTER EVENING CHRONICLE

The Deputy commissioner reported difficulties with the teleprinter system which repeatedly broke down because of over-load at Leyton Buzzard. It was suggested that there should be two separate channels for London and the south, and for Leeds and the north.

Beyond the doors were separate rest rooms for men and women along the corridor. A dart board could be seen in the men's, while the other had tea-making facilities. In another room, girls in blue overalls were on 24-hour rota duty at teleprinter machines. They were not permitted to read incoming messages; they had to call for the commanding officer.

At the end of the corridor was the emergency generator to ensure the lighting and the telephone never failed. Close by, higher up the wall, there was an emergency escape trapdoor which led outside the building.

The Map Room was entered off this passage. It was a long room painted in bright yellow, and most of the walls were covered with maps, right up to the ceiling. One map indicated where enemy action was taking place, another showed non-military incidents such as coal pit incidents or landslides. There were five partitioned telephone booths, with incoming calls being taken by other women in blue uniforms.

When an incident occurred, wardens filled in a report form and telephoned the details to the local control centre, which would notify the regional War Room. If telephone lines were down, dispatch riders, cyclists or runners were sent out to bring back first reports on major incidents. The War Room personnel would then inform the national headquarters at the War Room of the Ministry of Home Security about damage incurred.

Opposite top: Fighting map

Opposite below: Dispatch riders

Below: Night operations clerk plots air incidents on map

Below bottom: Control centre system

MANCHESTER EVENING CHRONICLE

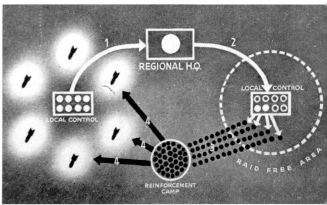

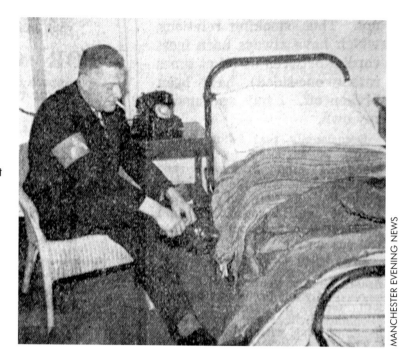

Right: Major Broadhurst in the office bedroom

On Burnage Lane, there were the offices of a firm of bakers. The firm was genuine but it hid a secret room, known as 'the room', below for plotting enemy aircraft. It was connected to outstations run by the Observer Corps and other services.

DONALD HENDERSON

The personnel were seated at two tables with the Chief of Staff, Major PGH Broadhurst, the Deputy Regional Commissioner, at the top of the room. The Major was a retired army officer and had been organising the ARP in the region. Over the heads of each of the people at the table was a job description - Plotting Officer, Records Clerk, the Operations Clerk and Operations Officer and the Intelligence Officer. All the personnel in the last two posts were professors from Manchester University. There were ten of them so that they could divide their time between their war duties and the university. The War Room staff had been trained at voluntary sessions three times a week for two hours.

Following a warning on the teleprinter, coloured disks were hung on hooks on a map of Britain divided into coded sections to denote the status of the alert and its location. Yellow was a warning, red meant raiders were overhead, green showed when the raiders had passed, and white was for all clear.

Warning of approaching raiders was also received by phone from the main telephone exchange. A large map of the North West on the wall, covered in coloured pins, represented every important facility in the region such as docks, factories and munition works. During an alert, a sheet of paper with the key to all these places and kept in a safe was pinned next to the map. As telephone reports come in via sub-control centres, coloured pins were placed on a larger three-section map of the region. A red pin represented a fire, yellow for gas and others for damaged bridges and roads. There was even a grey pin in case of civil disobedience. Each area was expected to deal with the emergency from its own resources, but if damages became

Top: Telephone operator receives message from the Chief of Staff

Below: Colonel T Blatherwick (left) Military Liaison Officer, and his two assistants Captain W Stott (centre) and Major TN Shelmerdine

too much to cope with, the War Room would organise help from outside areas. This method of receiving and recording information ensured an accurate picture of the situation was formed, and, if necessary reserves could be drafted in.

There were said to have been special sleeping quarters for Sir Winston Churchill in the command post but there is no information as to whether he used them. There was a bedroom at Arkwright House for the use of the Commissioner and his deputy during the early stages of the war.

One newspaper reporter wrote about going down many steps to the War Room, but plans of the building from 1935 show a basement and sub-basement. After the last war the building was used by the Department of Transport, and has since been substantially altered at basement level.

Arkwright House baement

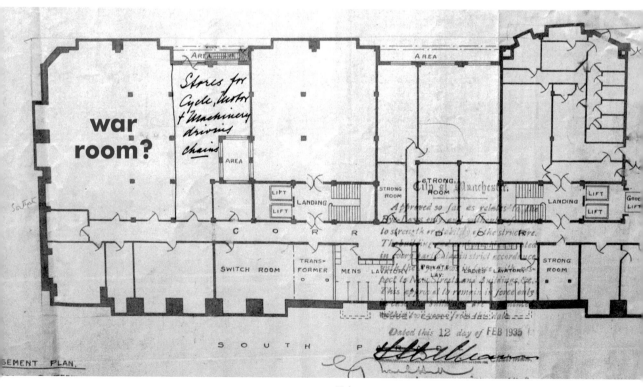

There were contingency plans to transfer the war room
to 'Heyscroft' off Palatine Road, Didsbury around 1942.
In readiness, the extensive basements had been
reinforced with steel girders and staff instructions issued.
The building was also used for ARP training, and was the
HQ of the auxiliary fire brigade. After the war it housed
the northwest training centre for the GPO.

MANCHESTER LIBRARIES

Regional War Room Staff regulations

REST DAYS
Each female member of the War Room Staff
has one rest day in four weeks.

RECREATION
Recreation is not allowed in the War Room,
but games may be played at suitable times
in the Games Room, subject to the Intelligence
Officer's permission.

SANITATION AND HYGIENE
The Logging Clerk of each team will see
that the War Room is sprayed with disinfectant
at least twice during their tour of duty.

The Supervisor of each team will see that telephone mouthpieces are cleansed with a solution
of Dettol as soon as possible after telephonists
come on duty.

OVERALLS - FEMALE STAFF
The Message Supervisor of each team should
ensure that each member of the team is provided
with overalls of the right size, and that each
member's initials (or name, if necessary) appears
boldly in marking ink in a central position at the
back of the overalls, under the collar.

It will be regarded as a strict breach of discipline
for any member of the teams to attempt to deface
or remove any member's name or initials.

GENERAL
Books, knitting, etc should not be left on the
telephone desk, but on the shelf provided for
that purpose.

WIRELESS BROADCAST RECEIVERS
A wireless set is maintained in the Map Room for
the reception of important announcements which
may be broadcast.

The Liaison Committee left to right:
Chief Superintendent Valentine,
Mr LF Field (Senior Regional Officer),
Colonel Blatherwick (Military Liaison
Officer), Miss Carey (Commissioner's
Private Secretary), Sir Warren Fisher,
Major Broadhurst

THE REGIONAL COMMISSIONERS

The North West, because of its importance during the war years as an industrial area and the port at Liverpool, was to have a series of distinguished Regional Commissioners and Deputies.

Sir Warren Fisher (April 1939 - May 1940) had been the Permanent Secretary to the Treasury and later became the first Head of the Civil Service, where he introduced many reforms. During his time as Regional Commissioner, he was an outspoken critic of Whitehall bureaucracy. His Deputies were JR Hobhouse (1939 - 1940), and Sir Thomas Blatherwick (1940 -1942), previously military liaison officer North West Region. Mr VR Kenny was Principal Officer (1939 - 1940), and Major PGH Broadhurst, Chief of Staff from 1939.

Sir Thomas Blatherwick's position as Deputy Regional Commissioner ended in 1942 when he was forced to resign by the Home Secretary Herbert Morrison and 'severely admonished'. Blatherwick had controversially allowed a fire service football team in Bolton to use their fire-tender to make the 278 mile round trip to a match with colleagues in Dumfries. This was criticised by some as an extravagant use of petrol in time of war. Subsequently fire-service vehicles were banned from attending sports meetings. In his defence, Blatherwick made the point that it was common practice to use the vehicles in this way, although he admitted it was an error of judgment to have used it on such a long journey.

His former boss, Sir Warren Fisher, got involved in the dispute over the dismissal. As a result of his typically forthright comments in a letter to the Guardian newspaper he was also forced to resign from his post as a Commissioner for the London region. Sir Warren, who had been head of the Civil Service for twenty years, questioned the Home Secretary's judgment on this matter, describing the sacking of Sir Thomas, who had an impressive record in public life as 'a gross injustice'. Blatherwick was born in Didsbury, and lived for many years in Knutsford, where he concluded his war service as Head Fire Guard. Later he was chairman of a number of organisations including the East Lancashire Territorial Army.

Sir Harry Haigh (May 1940 - January 1941) held various offices in the Indian Civil Service between 1925 and 1939 including Governor of the United Provinces. Haigh was appointed as Regional Commissioner for the Southern region in 1941.

Sir Aukland Campbell-Geddes (Lord Geddes) had served in David Lloyd George's coalition government during the First World War and had been the British Ambassador to the United States (1920-1924). He had been a Professor of Anatomy at various universities (1906-1914), President of the Board of Trade (1919-1920)

Top: Sir Harry Haigh inspecting American ambulances in Manchester

Below: Lord Geddes speaking to the Manchester Chamber of Commerce February 1939

GUARDIAN

Sir Aukland Geddes (right) with the Lord Mayor of Manchester, Alderman Wright Robinson

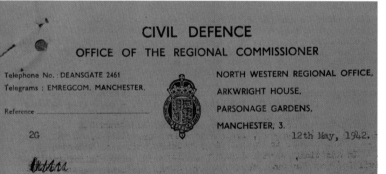

CIVIL DEFENCE

OFFICE OF THE REGIONAL COMMISSIONER

Telephone No. : DEANSGATE 2461

Telegrams : EMREGCOM, MANCHESTER.

Reference

2G

NORTH WESTERN REGIONAL OFFICE,

ARKWRIGHT HOUSE,

PARSONAGE GARDENS,

MANCHESTER, 3.

12th May, 1942.

as well as Chairman of several major companies. During WW2 he came out of retirement to be Regional Commissioner first in the South East, and then the North West (1 January 1941 - July 1942). Hartley Shawcross, who had been his Deputy in the South East region, said of Geddes 'he had one of the best minds I have encountered; he spoke thoughtfully, but with much assurance. He strode around the war room at our headquarters at Tunbridge Wells with its great map showing the air raid situation of the whole country in a notably deliberate way. You could not hurry him. And you could not ignore him.' Frederick Hindle was Geddes' Deputy in the North West from 1941.

Hartley Shawcross (July 1942 - March 1945) took over from Lord Geddes whose eyesight was failing. Shawcross was born in Germany in 1902 where his father was professor of English at Frankfurt University. He joined the Labour party at 16 and later studied law. He chaired the Enemy Aliens Tribunal (1941-1942) and was the Recorder of Salford (1941-1945). When he replaced Lord Geddes as Regional Commissioner a small bedroom was made at Arkwright House in order for him to remain close to his work. While shopping in Kendals, he over-heard someone say 'Look, that's the Regional Commissioner over there'. He was flattered to be recognised until the other person said ' Do you mean him that stands outside the Regal in the green uniform with silver braid?' By the time of his appointment, concern over invasion or air attack had receded and he was mainly involved in assisting the development of industrial production, visiting factories to give pep talks to the employees. After the war he was MP for St Helens and then achieved interna-tional fame when he led the British prosecu-tion at the Nuremberg Trials. He was involved in other high-profile cases including the prosecution of William Joyce (Lord Haw-Haw), traitor John Amery, acid bath murderer John George Haigh, and Klaus Fuchs the Atom bomb spy. Later he became a life peer and was on the board of a number of companies.

Shawcross had once been considered a potential prime minister but a series of undiplomatic remarks and disillusionment with Labour nationalisation policies ended his chance of high office. Liberals nicknamed him 'Sir Shortly Floorcross' because of his Tory leanings during the war years and he is reported to have described himself as a 'right-wing socialist'. Professor RST Chorley was the Deputy Regional Commissioner from 1942 to October 1944.

Hartley Shawcross

GUARDIAN

Basement Air-Raid Shelters

The City Architect surveyed 907 basements in the City which could be converted into public air raid shelters. They were classified as follows:

Class A. Basements in modern steel-framed buildings of more than four storeys with one or more concrete floors.

Class B. Basements in brick or steel-framed buildings, four or more storeys high with timber floors.

Class C. Basements in buildings up to four storeys high which could be made suitable at much higher cost than those in classes A and B.

It was estimated that shelter accommodation for around 200,000 people would be required and could be provided in A and B class basements at a cost of £600,000.

Manchester Corporation issued its first list of designated basement properties to be used as public air-raid shelters in August 1939, under the Civil Defence Act. This included a number of well-known buildings such as the Paramount Cinema, the Refuge Building and the Ryland building. Some of the 172 premises would need strengthening. It was estimated that 500 shelters would eventually be required for 100,000 people.

Appeals could be lodged if sent within fourteen days of receiving the notices. Companies feared that all of the basements would be required, but the authorities moved to reassure them that only sections of the basements were to be used, leaving the rest for their own staff and storage. The only grounds for appeal were if all the space was required for the protection of staff or if the work being done there was of national importance. It will be seen in the list following that many companies and organisations did successfully appeal against the notices, judging by the many gaps in the numbering of premises.

The shelters were planned to accommodate between 100 and 200 people, although these numbers were occasionally exceeded. Basements were to be strengthened with timber beams and props. The Home Office recommended iron and steel girders and sheeting but this was scarce.

The public shelters were intended as refuges for people caught in the street by a raid. People working in business premises had shelters provided by their employers.

GREATER MANCHESTER COUNTY RECORD OFFICE

It was known at the time that, despite all the preparations, a direct hit from a 500lb bomb could bring down a multi-storey building and explode in a basement. To be protected from this would require a shelter 60ft below ground with a 15ft-thick layer of concrete over the shelter. This was clearly not practicable and despite much debate about deep-level shelters, most of the population had to take their chances in basements or in small shelters at home.

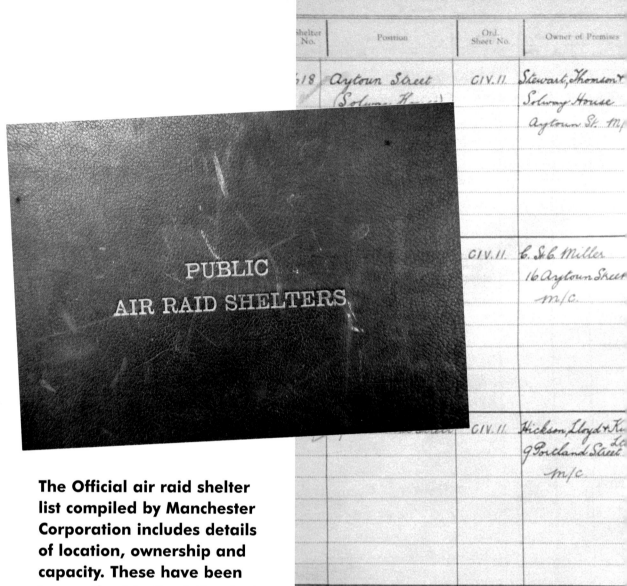

Shelter No.	Position	Ord. Sheet No.	Owner of Premises
618	Aytoun Street (Solway House)	CIV.11	Stewart, Thomson & Solway House Aytoun St. M/
		CIV.11	C. & C. Miller 16 Aytoun Street m/c.
		CIV.11	Hickson, Lloyd & Ky Ltd 9 Portland Street m/c
622	3 Portland Street	CIV.11	Hickson, Lloyd & K. 3/9 Portland Stre m/c
623	105 Princess Street	CIV.10	A. Haworth L 23 Strutt Stre m/c

The Official air raid shelter list compiled by Manchester Corporation includes details of location, ownership and capacity. These have been transcribed In the following pages.

The number of each shelter is shown but where there are gaps, this indicates properties originally listed, but later withdrawn because they were either privately used or were unsuitable.

3. 50 Granby Row
Owned by Sackville Estates Ltd
Capacity 200

5. Africa House, Whitworth Street
Owned by Lloyds Packing Warehouses
Capacity 176

7. Dominion House, Whitworth Street
Owned by Lloyds Packing Warehouses Ltd
Capacity 190

8. Refuge, Whitworth Street
Owned by Refuge Assurance Co Ltd
Capacity 150

9. Bridgewater House, Whitworth Street
Owned by Lloyds Packing Warehouses
Capacity 200

24. 86 Princess Street
Owned by Oxford Packing Co
Capacity 170

29. 118 Portland Street
Owned by G Benson & Son
Capacity 130

34. 106 Portland Street
Owned by Portland Buildings Ltd
Capacity 200

49. 88 Deansgate
Owned by Manchester Diocesan Church House Co
Capacity 200

51. 76 Deansgate
Owned by E W Hardy and Co
Capacity 360

52. 42 Deansgate
Owned by G Hardy and Co
Capacity 190

56. 118/124 Deansgate
Owned by Waring and Gillow Ltd
Capacity 200

57. 90 Deansgate
Owned by Manchester Diocesan Church House Co
Capacity 200

70. 205 Deansgate
Owned by Lancashire & Cheshire Band of Hope
Capacity 170

76. 123/5 Deansgate
Owned by Finnigans Ltd
Capacity 185

81. Market Street (Lyons)
Owned by J Lyons and Co Ltd
Capacity 200

85. 86 Market Street
Owned by The Times Furnishing Co Ltd
Capacity 200

89. 52/6 Market Street
Owned by Saxone Shoe Co Ltd
Capacity 190

92. 9/11 Oldham Street
Owned by John V Hutton Ltd
Capacity 140

93. 13/19 Oldham Street
Owned by C&A Modes Ltd
Capacity 200

Saxone, Market Street

94. 21 Oldham Street
Owned by Mr J Jones
Capacity 200

95. 35/43 Oldham Street
Owned by Pall Mall Property Co Ltd
Capacity 200

96. Oldham Street (Afflecks)
Owned by Affleck and Brown Ltd
Capacity 200

98. 47 Corporation Street
Owned by Van Den Berghs & Jurgens Ltd
Capacity 190

107. 57 Great Ancoats Street
Owned by J G Needham Ltd
Capacity 160

108. 11 Piccadilly
Owned by Littlewood Stores
Capacity 300

109. 35 Dale Street
Owned by R Haworth and Co Ltd
Capacity 200

112. 53 Dale Street
Owned by J D Williams and Co Ltd
Capacity 200

113. 49 Dale Street
Owned by W O'Hanlon and Co Ltd
Capacity 140

114. 57 Hilton Street
Owned by W O'Hanlon and Co Ltd
Capacity 200

COMMUNAL SHELTER AMENITIES
Users Must Provide Them

The Emergency Committee to the Manchester City Council in its monthly report deals with complaints that have been received to the effect that in the communal shelters there are no seating, lighting, and sanitary facilities.

The committee observes that having regard to the fact that communal shelters are only provided for eligible householders, where it is impossible to provide individual shelters, and as individual shelters have no such facilities, the Home Office considers that the persons entitled to the use of the communal shelters should provide anything more which they consider to be necessary, the contention being that the shelters are situated sufficiently close to the houses which they are intended to serve to enable the occupants of the shelters to take such facilities with them.

Accordingly the committee has no authority to provide seating, lighting, or sanitary facilities in communal shelters. Some misconception as to the position has arisen owing to the fact that before the Home Office issued specific instructions on the subject certain of these shelters were provided with the facilities referred to.

Wesley Hall, Gt Ancoats Street

115. 32 Hilton Street
Owned by W O'Hanlon and Co Ltd
Capacity 200

124. 19/25 Piccadilly
Owned by F W Woolworth and Co
Capacity 165

126. Great Ancoats Street (Wesley Hall)
Owned by Thomas Davies (President)
Capacity 200

131. 109 Piccadilly
Owned by City Properties (M/c)
Capacity 579

132. 107 Piccadilly
Owned by Horrockses, Crewdson and Co
Capacity 200

140. 3 Chepstow Street
Owned by Booth and Others Ltd
Capacity 175

141. 28 Oxford Street
Owned by Booth and Others Ltd
Capacity 180

142. 16 Oxford Street (Mecca Cafe)
Owned by Batey, Markham and Heywood
Capacity 200

146. 76 Great Bridgewater Street
Owned by Greenough, Occleston and Co
Capacity 200

151. 28 Quay Street
Owned by Simpson & Godlee Ltd
Capacity 200

155. King Street West
Owned by The Wallpaper Manufacturer Ltd
Capacity 185

156. 11 Peter Street
W H Sutton and Co
Capacity 180

158. 44 Peter Street
Owned by J Line and Sons
Capacity 200

160. 37 Peter Street
Owned by Fothergill and Harvey Ltd
Capacity 200

161. YMCA Peter Street
Owned by YMCA
Capacity 150

165. St Mary's Parsonage
Owned by National Boiler and General Association
Capacity 200

168. Middleton Road (Smithfields)
Owned by H and J Bradshaw
Capacity 200

169. Cateaton and Victoria Street
Owned by W H Sutton and Sons
Capacity 200

180. 36 Queen Street
Part owned by G H Shahbenderian
Capacity 125

182. 7 Brazennose Street
Owned by Hall, Bryden and Chapman
Capacity 190

Food in Raid Shelters

With the sanction of the Ministry of Food arrangements have been made in Manchester for supplying light refreshments to people in air-raid shelters during the forthcoming winter.

Mr J Foley, head of the city's Food Control Department told a reporter that the arrangements covered about eight large shelters in the city. The service was in no sense to be a trading enterprise; it should be undertaken by voluntary bodies who had been given facilities to obtain supplies. Smaller shelters, he added, would be served by organisations which run mobile canteens.

Light refreshments only, including hot drinks, will be supplied to shelterers on a non-profit-making basis. The service is a development from beginnings made by local committees last winter.

Guardian September 1941

Gaoled after scene at raid shelter

A scene at an air raid shelter in Manchester had a sequel at the Manchester City Police Court to-day when Christopher Leigh (50), of Daniel-street, Hulme, Manchester, was sent to prison for two months.

Leigh was charged with being drunk and assaulting a police officer.

A detective said he went to the shelter after receiving a complaint from a warden. There he saw people shouting and children crying. Outside the shelter Leigh was shouting and apparently wanting to fight.

The officer added that he took Leigh into custody, and was kicked on the legs. A sergeant of the Home Guard had to help him.

186. Rusholme Road
Owned by Exors of C Slater
Capacity 200

187. 12 Ducie Street (Longsight)
Owned by James Dyson (M/c) Ltd
Capacity 175

190. Renshaw and South Streets
Owned by Hardy's Crown Brewery Co Ltd
Capacity 200

193. 58 Stockport Road
Owned by J Collier and Co Ltd
Capacity 60

194. Stockport Road-Grey Street
Owned by British Vinegars Ltd
Capacity 200

200. Worsley Street (Premier Box)
Owned by Tillotson and Son Ltd
Capacity 175

207. 57 Dale Street
Owned by F W Millington
Capacity 200

209. 29 & 31 Dale Street
Owned by Pugh Davies and Co Ltd
Capacity 360

212. 76/80 Oldham Street
Owned by Dobbins Ltd
Capacity 175

215. 55/61 Lever Street
Owned by Abel Heywood and Son Ltd
Capacity 200

219. 84 Boardman Street
Owned by David Moseley and Sons
Capacity 180

220. 92 Tipping Street
Owned by C W Provis and Son
Capacity 110

229. Fairfield Street (Yates)
Owned by Exors of C Slater
Capacity 125

230. Princess Street (Chesters)
Owned by Chesters Brewery Ltd
Capacity 200

234. 235 Wilmslow Road
Owned by M/c and Salford Co-op Society
Capacity 60

242. 30a Mason Street
Owned by Mall-Max Hat Co Ltd
Capacity 150

244. 45 Goulden Street
Owned by Marsden, Harcombe and Co
Capacity 175

247. 19 Birch Street
Owned by Palatine Bottling
Capacity 200

248. Lower Ormond Street (PAC)
Owned by Public Assistance Committee
Capacity 90

249. Higher Ormond Street (Rightons)
Owned by W Righton Ltd
Capacity 200

Rightons, Higher Ormond St

252. Stretford Road (Zion)
Owned by Zion Congregational Church
Capacity 200

255. Ackers Place
Owned by Burgons Ltd
Capacity 200

278. Oldham Road (St Pauls)
Owned by Rev E Gowing
Capacity 200

279. 44 Addington Street
Owned by John Battersby and Son
Capacity 200

282. Rochdale Road (Veritas House)
Owned by Falk, Stadelmann & Co
Capacity 200

284. 20 Swan Street
Owned by J Lingard and Sons
Capacity 180

285. 7 Gt Ancoats Street
Owned by Gallahers Ltd
Capacity 200

288. 11 Albert Square
Owned by Ellerman and Papayanni Lines Ltd
Capacity 200

294. 15 Tib Street
Owned by Rylands and Sons Ltd
Capacity 200

295. 31/3 Church Street
Owned by Exors of C Slater
Capacity 200

Veritas House, Rochdale Road

300. Rusholme Road (Congregational Church)
Owned by Hon Sec G Kelly
Capacity 200

301. 22 St Lukes Street
Owned by Exors of Thos Clapham
Capacity 200

306. 53 Fountain Street
Owned by J T Lewis and Co
Capacity 200

308. Oxford Hall, Oxford Road
Owned by Manchester & Salford Methodist Mission
Capacity 200

315. 4 Trumpet Street
Owned by Manchester Guardian & Evening News
Capacity 200

316. 8 City Road
Owned by H H Pearlberg
Capacity 200

330. Dyer Street, Hulme
Owned by W Mather Ltd
Capacity 170

331. Mulberry Street
Owned by Lord Mayor's Unemployment Committee
Capacity 200

333. Erskine Street
Owned by Grove and Whitnall Ltd
Capacity 200

339. 6 Beaver Street
Owned by Manchester Central Packing
Capacity 160

'During the last three weeks I have had the privilege of visiting many of these (mill) shelters at night during air-raids. Without exception I have found the people, men and women and mothers with little children most courteous, patient and cheerful. To sit for long hours in these places at night would test fairly severely the tempers of even the best of us.'

VICAR

Guardian September 1940

'To sit for long hours in these places at night would test fairly severely the tempers of even the best of us.'

Overleaf: City centre public air-raid shelters

The Not-So-Easy Chair

The 'Lancet' notes the appearance of a new shelter ailment which at least has the merit of not being contagious. Unlike colds, tonsillitis, or shelter throat 'shelter legs' cannot be caught by one sufferer to another. The patient, usually of the older and heavier type consults the doctor for swelling and soreness in the legs, and it is usually found that he or she has been spending night after night in a deck-chair the wooden cross-bar of which 'causes pressure on the back of the thigh or 'on the popliteal vessels.' The deck-chair, a good friend in gardens or on sunshine cruises, is revealed as an inadequate substitute for bed - a discovery which has probably been made by a good many people during recent months and without the necessity of a visit to the doctor. It was never, perhaps, quite so comfortable a seat as it was supposed to be; unless it was so adjusted that the sitters feet were firmly on the ground (in which case it had no special advantages over an ordinary chair) there was bound to be pressure from that cross-bar which would be plainly felt after an prolonged session. Probably its associations with sunshine and fresh air imparted a tradition of ease and well-being that the structure itself never really deserved. 'Shelter legs' can be cured by avoiding the seat which causes them. It will be odd if the deck-chair itself never recovers from the shadow which the air-raid shelter has cast upon it.

Guardian December 1940

340. Junction Street (Naval Brewery)
Owned by J G Swales and Co Ltd, Hulme
Capacity 175

341. 64 Bridge Street
Owned by Rational Assurance Friendly Society
Capacity 190

342. Bridge Street (Masonic Temple)
Owned by Masonic Club Masonic Temple
Capacity 200

343. 101 Portland Street
Owned by Fraser and Son
Capacity 200

347. 28 Canal Street
Owned by R Fitton Ltd
Capacity 200

348. 54 Princess Street
Owned by Bronnert and Co
Capacity 300

349. 3 Dale Street
Owned by C B and W Lenthall
Capacity 200

350. 20 Dale Street
Owned by Marshall and Aston Ltd
Capacity 200

360. 45 Chorlton Street
Owned by Ashton and Co
Capacity 150

361. 4 Canal Street
Owned by M Nairn and Co
Capacity 85

366. 23 Pall Mall
Owned by London Assurance
Capacity 120

367. Hyde Road (Beswick Co-op)
Owned by The Beswick Co-op
Capacity 185

369. 12 York Street
Owned by Railton and Knowles
Capacity 130

376. 29 Pall Mall
Owned by J Ringrose and Co
Capacity 200

390. 31 Erskine Street (Hulme)
Owned by R Gibson and Sons
Capacity 200

392. 15 Birch Street (Hulme)
Owned by Hamlin and Co
Capacity 170

397. 14 Bridge Street
Owned by Lloyds Packing Warehouses Ltd
Capacity 175

408. Little Lever Street (Houldsworth House)
Owned by W H Robinson and Co
Capacity 160

416. 40 Bloom Street
Owned by G H Taylor and Son
Capacity 130

420. Moss Lane West (Hydes Brewery)
Owned by Hydes Queens Brewery Ltd
Capacity 125

Manchester Corporation took over most of the basement of the Mulberry Bush Club in Hulme which had been used as a canteen. Refreshments and entertainment such as film shows and gramophone concerts were provided. It was used each time by around 200 people who brought their own bedding and slept on forms and on the concrete floor. Mothers brought their children between 5.30pm and 6pm, with the fathers coming in later after work for their evening meal. After the canteen closed at 10.30, children helped to wash the pots and tidy the canteen. Lights were out by 10.45pm.

GUARDIAN

Slacks and sweater form a practical outfit.

424. 35 High Street
Owned by Joseph and Thorpe
Capacity 200

425. 39 High Street
Owned by Joseph and Thorpe
Capacity 100

426. 12-16 Church Street
Owned by P Lloyd Rees Ltd
Capacity 100

427. 24 Church Street
Owned by The Pall Mall Property Co
Capacity 130

428. 26 Oldham Street
Owned by Jays Furnishing Stores
Capacity 190

432. 22 Oldham Street
Owned by Prudential Assurance Co
Capacity 125

434. 31 Quay Street
Owned by T Westbrook
Capacity 125

437. Jackson Street (Spinning Co)
Owned by Fine Cotton Spinners
and Doublers Association
Capacity 200

441/2. Gt Jackson Street - City Road
Owned by Manchester Trades Supply Co Ltd
Capacity 200

453. Wilmslow Road (District Bank)
Owned by District Bank Ltd
Capacity 80

455. 76 Victoria Street
Owned by Railton and Knowles
Capacity 100

457. 20 Duke Street - Bridgewater Street
Owned by J Cookson Ltd
Capacity 180

458. 65 High Street
Owned by W Sutcliffe Ltd
Capacity 200

460. 51 York Street
Owned by Executors of Samuel Sidebottom
Capacity 200

465. 120 Rusholme Road
Owned by Amalgamated Engineering Union
Capacity 130

466. Grosvenor Street (Oddfellows)
Owned by Manchester Unity of Oddfellows
Capacity 80

474. 18 Tomlinson Street
Owned by Cawood, Dyson and Co
Capacity 180

478. Wilmslow Road (Presby. Church)
Owned by Withington Presby. (C of E)
Capacity 140

480. Chapman Street (Popular Cinema)
Owned by Popular Picture Palaces of (Hulme) Ltd
Capacity 200

482. 148 Princess Street
Owned by Shaws Buildings Ltd
Capacity 150

'The most important thing about raid technique is to eat, sleep, dress and shelter in the same place. Gradually therefore, a technique is being developed in which the provision of suitable clothing plays an important part. Those who still have to go out to their shelter find the siren suit, whether merely trousers and sweater or more subtle creations, the most useful for sitting about and sleeping.'

Guardian December 1940
(See opposite page)

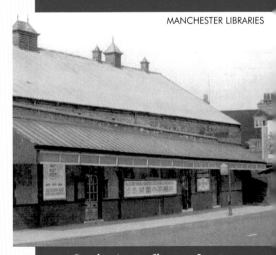

Popular cinema, Chapman Street

484. Brook Street (J Noble)
Owned by John Noble Ltd
Capacity 200

494. 2-4 London Road
Owned by E R Buck and Sons
Capacity 170

499. 46/50 Oldham Street
Owned by Marks and Spencer Ltd
Capacity 200

500. 36/38 Church Street
Owned by Bathop Taylor and Ogden
Capacity 200

502. 21 Lever Street
Owned by J R Bridgford and Sons
Capacity 180

There were basement shelters in both the Town Hall and Extension. The ceilings and walls were strengthened and employees could be directed in safety from one building to the other via the Lloyd Street subway.

KNOW THESE SIGNALS

POLICE WHISTLES / WAVERING SIREN — **RAID – TAKE COVER**

RATTLE — **GAS-MASKS ON**

STEADY SIREN NOTE — **RAIDERS PASSED** but gas may still be about

HANDBELLS — **ALL CLEAR**

CHURCH BELLS — **PARACHUTE TROOPS** keep calm, hide maps, disable your car, tell the police quickly and accurately if you see NAZIS.

504. 75 Piccadilly
Owned by J Chorlton and Sons
Capacity 150

505. 7/9 Piccadilly
Owned by J Lyons and Co Ltd
Capacity 200

512. Briddon Street (Strangeways)
Owned by Boddington Brewery
Capacity 200

517. 5 Zinc Street
Owned by M Brodie and Son Ltd
Capacity 140

518. Oxford Street (Odeon)
Owned by Odeon Theatres Ltd
Capacity 200

519. 22 Dickenson Street
Owned by Paramount Film Services Ltd
Capacity 150

521. 22 Wilbraham Road
Owned by Chorlton Conservative Club
Capacity 85

524. 2 Roby Street
Owned by W B and M Ashworth
Capacity 175

530. 42 Charles Street
Owned by J and J Shaw Ltd
Capacity 160

546. 5 Cross Street
Owned by A Haworth Ltd
Capacity 200

22 Wilbraham Road

551. Chester Street and Cambridge Street
Owned by A Megson and Son Ltd
Capacity 200

555. London Road (Gas Meter Testing Station)
Owned by Clerk to Justices
Capacity 320

560. 1-2 North Parade, Deansgate
Owned by Independent Order of Rechabites
Capacity 125

561. 67 Shudehill
Owned by Thomas Hudson's Executors Ltd
Capacity 200

566. 10 Marsden Street
Owned by S C Chorlton
Capacity 200

568. 27/31 Minshull Street
Owned by A Hughes and Co Ltd
Capacity 110

569. 16 Chepstow Street
Owned by Barlows Ltd
Capacity 200

573. 31 Pollard Street
Owned by Thomas Hope Ltd
Capacity 175

576. Monsall Road (Wilson's Brewery)
Owned by Wilson's Brewery Ltd
Capacity 200

580. 1 Whalley Road
Owned by Mr A S Burd
Capacity 130

588. 38 Whitworth Street
Owned by Whitworth and Mitchell
Capacity 200

590. 68/72 Great Ducie Street
Owned by W Timpson Ltd
Capacity 200

602. 9 Gore Street
Owned by Joshua Hoyle and Son
Capacity 200

609. 39 Great Ducie Street
Owned by J Cockshoot and Co
Capacity 200

615. 16 Queen Street
Owned by District Prov. and Charity
Organization of Manchester and Salford
Capacity 200

618. Aytoun Street (Solway House)
Owned by Stewart, Thomson and Co
Capacity 175

619. 16 Aytoun Street
Owned by C S C Miller
Capacity 200

621. 9 Portland Street
Owned by Hickson, Lloyd and King
Capacity 200

622. 3 Portland Street
Owned by Hickson, Lloyd and King
Capacity 200

623. 105 Princess Street
Owned by A Haworth Ltd
Capacity 200

The decision of the Manchester Emergency Committee to prohibit lectures organised by the WEA youth groups raises the whole question of shelter activities. May I take for instance, the case of our public shelter? Our greatest problem is what to do for the adolescents. Every night numbers of youths and girls congregate in the shelter and remain there throughout the evening, and that is still true even in the lighter evenings. They never read, the girls never knit, and unless we can help them they simply stand about and gossip and make themselves a general nuisance to everyone. The obvious although by no means easy solution is to find them some occupation. This we have tried to do.

Throughout the winter months we run games evenings for the children, and clubs (with games, elocution, singing, drill) for the young people. In addition to this we have had musical evenings, community singing, concerts, films, travel talks, and lantern lectures, and here our best help has come from the WEA. Lantern lectures, including one by Captain Shawcross on the merchant navy, several on travel, and one by members of the YHA. Normally anything suggestive of education would antagonise these young folk at once, but from sheer boredom they have been willing to listen. Moreover, they have listened well and have come again to the next lecture.

Rev G R Myers,
The Oxford Hall, Oxford Road
Guardian 1 April 1941

Shelter basement, 55 Piccadilly
Manchester Corporation Transport
Department offices

Manchester Royal Infirmary had
nine basement shelters. They were
intentionally spread around the
hospital grounds so that medical
personnel were not concentrated
in one area. They all had bunks
and mattresses and were supervised
by wardens. They were also used by
outpatients. The Nurses' Home building received a direct hit in December
1940. None of the 112 nurses in the
shelter below was injured, but the
buildings were badly damaged.

630. Junction and Ducie Street
Owned by Lingard and Wright
Capacity 200

632/3. 37 Ducie Street
Owned by G J Fletcher
Capacity 160

641. 32/40 Portland Street
Owned by A and S Henry and Co Ltd
Capacity 200

652. 9a Nicholas Street
Owned by Heywood, Son and Hudson
Capacity 150

654. 12 Charlotte Street
Owned by Langworthy Brothers and Co
Capacity 200

655. 1 Dickenson Street West
Owned by J Wainwright and Son
Capacity 200

661. 8 Minshull Street
Owned by A Haworth Ltd
Capacity 200

664. 66 Mosley Street
Owned by Earl's Estates
Capacity 200

665. 1 Cooper Street
Owned by Miller Speakman and Hall
Capacity 200

677. 69/71 Mosley Street
Owned by Pye and Bennett
Capacity 200

Extracts from an investigation by women doctors into the conditions in air-raid shelters in Hulme and north Manchester

'One is under a church. The people arrive from 6pm onwards. At 11 pm there were between 20-30 adults and children who had come for the night. They were sitting upright on benches, leaning against the wall, and had not begun to retire. While soundly constructed, this shelter was cold, and this was the main complaint. It was lit by electricity, but there was no lighting in the women's lavatories and no privacy. It must be extremely difficult to clean out the lavatories in the absence of lighting, and very difficult for children to use for the same reason. It was stated that mothers come from considerable distances to this shelter to have the advantage of the wooden floor for their children to sleep on. There is no sick bay and no one in charge except during raids. There are insufficient forms to seat the 350 persons who arrive during raids.

A basement shelter in Miles Platting was bad in every respect. At 10.50pm about fifty persons had arrived for the night, including many small children. Only about twenty persons had retired. Eleven children were sleeping on the concrete floor, two of these had a piece of plywood between them and the floor, the rest were lying on thin wraps. A few of the children were sleeping on forms. One family of three wide-awake babies were all coughing, and on enquiry, the mother said that they had been sleeping in the shelter for the last three months. All the children were incredibly dirty and tired-looking. The supports and ceiling are of timber and provide a source of danger from fire. One group of persons was observed crowding round a candle under a flower-pot as a source of heating. The floor was of concrete and was very wet near both emergency exits, where sawdust has been supplied to combat the dampness. A second source of damp was present near the women's toilets, and it was stated that this came from the overflow or misuse. Three of the occupants, including the shelter marshal were interviewed separately, and stated that the closets were not emptied daily and that the cleaning of the shelter was done through the public-spiritedness of two of the women. The ladders leading to emergency exits were steep and led to trap doors, both of which opened inwards. There is no official warden for the shelter. There is a room for first-aid, but there was no one present who was either trained or capable of exerting any authority.

A good mill shelter

In contrast the third shelter was situated under a mill. It had been organised for the use of its operatives during daytime raids, and was available for local people at night. This shelter was clean, warm and quiet. Beds were provided, and at 11pm, all the occupants had retired and nearly all were asleep and the electric lighting had been dimmed. It has an excellent sick bay, well equipped, well lit and warm, and three of the mill employees, trained in first aid were in attendance. The sanitary arrangements were adequate and private. The shelter is heated from the mill and hot water for tea was available. This was the only shelter in which by far the majority of the occupants were asleep, in spite of a large proportion of babies, and demonstrates the necessity for beds, dimmed lights, and quiet, and the advantages of supervision.'

GUARDIAN

the air problem in the
AIR-RAID SHELTER

The crowds that fill Air Raid Shelters must always include a number of persons who are carriers of infection. The longer and more frequently the shelters are occupied, therefore, the more favourable become conditions for air-borne infection.

As winter approaches, the number of carriers of infection will increase. The possibility that the shelters may become focal points of infection will become greater still.

That is the problem which faces Public Health Authorities, industrial concerns and householders alike.

and its solution

This problem can be solved quickly and effectively by:—

(a) the spraying of the shelter air at regular intervals with a dilute solution of Izal Germicide in the form of a fine mist.

(b) the periodic cleansing of shelter walls, seats and floors with the same solution.

Most air-borne germs are carried by dust. A mist spray of Izal solution in addition to its exceptional germicidal power has greater wetting power than plain water. It bears to the ground the dust suspended in the air, at the same time destroying any harmful germs. The spray, though it does not make the shelter damp, leaves a thin film of Izal on the floor, walls and seats, destroying germs and assisting in keeping down dust. The Izal spray has other important advantages. It stimulates the nasal passages and helps to increase the resistance of the individual to infection. The "freshening" effect of the spray on vitiated air is particularly noticeable during long periods of occupation. Where spraying with Izal has already been adopted, it has been greatly appreciated by the public.

PLEASANT SMELLS DO NOT KILL GERMS!

678. 6 Booth Street
Owned by Pye and Bennett
Capacity 185

682. 17A Nicholas Street
Owned by Executors of Louis Schwate
Capacity 170

690. 35 Whitworth Street
Owned by Lloyds Packing Warehouse Co Ltd
Capacity 160

691. 17 Whitworth Street West
Owned by William Thompson and Co Ltd
Capacity 200

694. Whitworth Street West (Ritz)
Owned by Ritz Palais de Danse Manchester L
Capacity 120

698. 82 George Street
Owned by J Teggin and Sons
Capacity 130

700. 86 George Street
Owned by A K Dyson and Co Ltd
Capacity 115

703. Mosley Street (Portico Library)
Owned by The Portico Library
Capacity 200

707. 32 Lees Street West (Ancoats)
Owned by Trotter, Davies and Yeasley
Capacity 200

753. 42 Bloom Street
Owned by Abraham Haworth
Capacity 200

756. 16a Nicholas Street West (Ritz)
Owned by J Alker and Co
Capacity 200

759. 38 Faulkner Street
Owned by T A and H Basley
Capacity 120

768. 34 Charlotte Street
Owned by J R Bridgford and Sons
Capacity 200

779. 36 Charlotte Street
Owned by Bank of London and South America Ltd
Capacity 200

780. 18 Booth Street
Owned by G H Bailey
Capacity 200

782. 1 Booth Street
Owned by Manchester Commercial Buildings Co
Capacity 200

783. 15 Cross Street (Bodega Restaurant)
Owned by Manchester Commercial Buildings Co
Capacity 200

788. Deansgate (Milton Hall)
Owned by The Governors,
Congregational Church House
Capacity 200

789. 2 St John Street
Owned by Longden and Sutcliffe
Capacity 175

793. 17 Hanover Street
Owned by CWS Ltd
Capacity 200 - *SEE CO-OP TUNNELS CHAPTER*

MANCHESTER LIBRARIES

2 St John's Street

827. 14 Charlotte Street
Owned by J Neild, Son and Lees
Capacity 180

845. 113 Newton Street
Owned by Mr G Petts and Co Ltd
Capacity 140

848. 47 Houldsworth Street
Owned by J Rostron and Sons Ltd
Capacity 165

858. 72 Newton Street
Owned by J H Norris and Sons
Capacity 150

864. 52a Newton Street
Owned by J H Norris and Sons
Capacity 200

873. 11 Stevenson Square
Owned by W H Robinson and Co
Capacity 200

902. 1 Newton Street
Owned by R C Stonex and Sons
Capacity 140

904. 15 Newton Street
Owned by Turner Coy and Jones
Capacity 120

907. 4 Little Lever Street
Owned by Webb and Hall
Capacity 200

910. 81 King Street (Reform Club)
Owned by Reform Club Building Co
Capacity 200

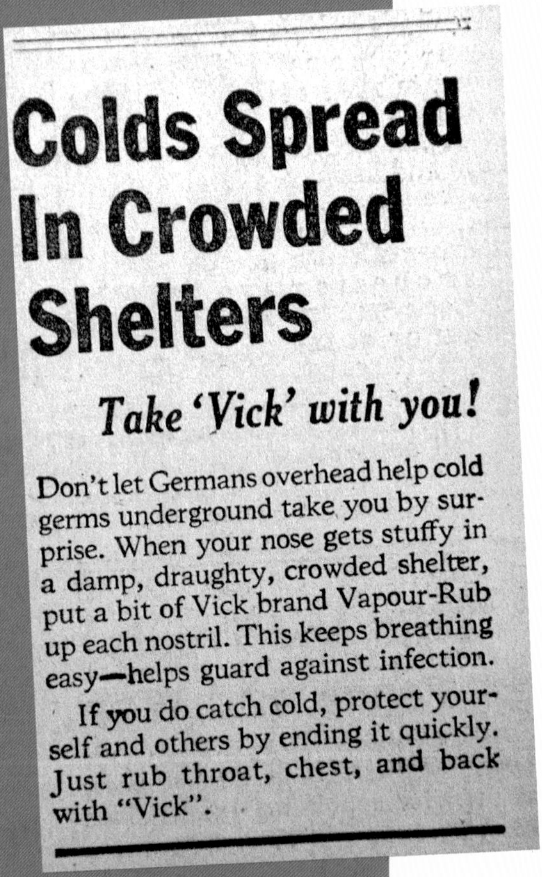

Colds Spread In Crowded Shelters

Take 'Vick' with you!

Don't let Germans overhead help cold germs underground take you by surprise. When your nose gets stuffy in a damp, draughty, crowded shelter, put a bit of Vick brand Vapour-Rub up each nostril. This keeps breathing easy—helps guard against infection.

If *you* do catch cold, protect yourself and others by ending it quickly. Just rub throat, chest, and back with "Vick".

911. 10/20 Thomas Street
Owned by H Matthews and Son
Capacity 145

919. 34 Cannon Street
Owned by W Briggs and Co Ltd
Capacity 100

922. St Peter's Square (Century House)
Owned by Friends Provident Society
Capacity 180

923. 40 Dickenson Street
Owned by Lloyds Packing Warehouses Ltd
Capacity 170

924. 8/11 Deansgate Arcade
Owned by Dendy and Patterson
Capacity 200

926. Cannon Street (Regent House)
Owned by Longden and Sutcliffe
Capacity 100

928. 399 Oldham Road
Owned by Humphrey, Watts and Fitups
Capacity 170

930. 284 Oldham Road
Owned by W Shufflebottom
Capacity 150

932. 25 Portland Street
Owned by Withington, Petty and Co
Capacity 200

933. 4 Chorlton Street
Owned by Withington, Petty and Co
Capacity 200

Top: St Peter's House
Below: Deansgate Arcade

Egerton Hall, Oxford Place

942. Oxford Place (Egerton Hall)
Owned by Rev K V Ramsey, Egerton Hall
Capacity 200

943. 421 Cheetham Hill Road
Owned by The United Society of Engravers
Capacity 145

944. 38 Deansgate
Owned by Scottish Life Assurance Co
Capacity 200

945. 755 Ashton Old Road (Crossley Lads Club)
Owned by Executors of Sir William Crossley.
Crossley Brothers
Capacity 130

947. 131 Cheetham Hill Road
Owned by Nathan Laski and Hyman
Capacity 200

950. Oak Drive, Fallowfield (Beechwood)
Owned by Typographical Association
Capacity 200

951. Ashton Old Road (Droylsden Co-op)
Owned by Droylsden Co-op Industrial Society
Capacity 200

952. Ashton Old Road (Berwick Co-op)
Owned by Berwick Co-op Industrial Society
Capacity 200

954. 14 Clarence Street, Cheetham
Owned by Mr R Marks
Capacity 200

955. Derby Street and Sherbourne Street
Owned by M Fidler and Co Ltd
Capacity 400

958. Mosley Street (Art Gallery)
Owned by Art Galleries Committee
Capacity 200

960. 7 Dale Street
Owned by I J and G Cooper Ltd
Capacity 180

961. 23 Cumberland Street
Owned by Austin House Co Ltd
Capacity 200

962. 14 The Parsonage, Ormes Buildings
Owned by Ormes Properties Ltd
Capacity 200

964. Great Southern Street
Owned by Smart Brothers Ltd
Capacity 200

968. St Peter's Square (Library)
Owned by Libraries Committee
Capacity 400

969. 13 East Street
Owned by Refuge Assurance Co
Capacity 200

971. Hyde Road, Belle Vue
Owned by Belle Vue (M/c) Ltd
Capacity 300

972. Oldham Road (Independent Chapel)
Owned by The Deacons of Manchester
Capacity 180

The glass dome of Central Library was boarded over on the outside, stack windows were blacked out and we scuttled in and out of our dim warren, like rabbits. Manchester was crowded with soldiers and airmen from all the countries of occupied Europe. Also, we had the Americans. Most young women were enamoured of the Poles (who haunted the entrance to Van Dock). They all seemed to be tall, blonde, handsome, quite mad and incredibly persistent.

We had a large public air-raid shelter in the perimeter of Stack 4, into which these troops crowded. The major concern of the Duty Officer during a night-time raid was not the threatening might of Germany but to prevent the prostitutes who normally plied their trade in Oxford Street from plying it in his shelter instead.

(Elizabeth Leach, former member of staff)

It is thought that the cellars used as shelters at Belle Vue were once used to take cash and other valuables from one part of the site to another. These 'secret underground chambers' as described in a newspaper article were between the Hyde Road entrance and the ballroom.

Friends Meeting House

The Mount Street shelter in the sub-basement was Manchester's first public air-raid shelter. It was described as 'gas and splinter proof' and opened in February 1938 as a model for later shelters. Windows and vents were sealed with hessian removed from the lining of tea-chests. Cracks in walls were covered in waterproof paper. There were forms and tables, water for drinking and washing, and toilets. Blankets and first-aid boxes and lanterns in case of electricity failure were also available. In case of falling debris, there were tools to clear blockages to the exit. There was also an emergency exit with a two-blanket airlock.

974. Hulme Hall Road (Terres Factory)
Owned by Holmes Terry and Co
Capacity 200

975. Mount Street (Friends Meeting House)
Owned by The Society of Friends
Capacity 190

977. 87 Rochdale Road
Owned by J Barlow and Sons Ltd
Capacity 180

978. 48 King Street
Owned by S Kershaw and Sons
Capacity 115

979. Turner Street (Clydesdale House)
Owned by E Dawson
Capacity 200

980. 19 George Street
Owned by Hall and Co
Capacity 200

981. 219/221 Chorlton Road
Owned by Miss Helena Harris
Capacity 150

982. Cavendish Street - Oxford Road
Owned by G Hardy and Co
Capacity 200

983. Oak House, Oak Drive
Owned by Edwin Jones
Capacity 200

984. 20 Every Street
Owned by Manchester University Settlement
Capacity 200

985. Palmerston Street (Ardwick Lads Club)
Owned by Noel Timpson
Capacity 110

987. 99 Hyde Road
Owned by S A Rhodes Ltd
Capacity 100

988. 17 Chorlton Street
Owned by W H Robinson and Co
Capacity 200

989. 184 Stockport Road
Owned by Croft and Marlow
Capacity 200

Ardwick Lads Club

990. Stockport Road (Longsight Library)
Owned by Libraries Committee
Capacity 100

992. Stretford Road (Hulme Town Hall)
Owned by Manchester Corporation
Capacity 200

993. Stockport Road (Levenshulme Town Hall)
Owned by Town Hall Committee
Capacity 150

994. 109 Portland Street
Owned by J Alker and Co
Capacity 200

995. 9 Lower Mosley Street
Owned by T A and H Barley
Capacity 400

996. 29 Blossom Street
Owned by Manchester Fish and Meat Salesmen's Ice Co Ltd
Capacity 175

A filthy shelter

This report was compiled by a corporation official following a visit by Ellen Wilkinson, Parliamentary Secretary to the Ministry of Home Security, to Manchester, in December 1940. Her slogan for better shelters was 'Safety, Sanitation, Sleep' and these observations highlight the problems in maintaining a well run, clean and hygienic communal shelter:

'The air-raid shelter is cleansed every morning. The pails are emptied and recharged with fluid disinfectant. The floors are swept with soft brushes and all rubbish taken away. Four men and one motor freighter are engaged on this shelter for one hour daily. Many people who use this shelter are filthy in their habits, and every morning the shelter is strewn with all kinds of rubbish.

It is a common occurrence for the men on this work to find empty beer bottles and milk bottles lying in the shelter, also tea leaves thrown on the floor. On the morning of December 4 (the morning after Miss Wilkinson's visit) the following articles were left scattered about the shelter: four flock beds, two pillows (one coat dirty and wet), four carpets, seven old coats for bed coverings, two old broken basket chairs, and one old home-made hearthrug.

There is evidence that small children are using corners of the shelters instead of the pails. There is always a number of cigarette ends lying about the shelter although smoking is not allowed. About four times a week full toilet rolls are found in the pails, and it is evident that the children using this shelter are doing a great deal of damage.

Ellen Wilkinson

It has been ascertained from the senior warden this morning that this shelter used to be one of the cleanest in this area. Children of all ages are sent there about 7.30pm, and use the shelter as a playground, upsetting all the work of cleansing which has taken place during the morning. Parents arrive at all hours of the night and early morning. There are two distinct types of people using this shelter: those who appreciate what is being done for them and who complain of the conduct of others, and those who conduct themselves badly. The better type of people referred to have formed themselves into a committee, and now work on a rota system to clean the place each morning.'

997. 8a Oxford Road (Regal Buildings)
Owned by Ogdens Theatres
Capacity 200

999. Cannon Street (Late Wilton Hotel)
Owned by City Surveyor
Capacity 200

1000. Cannon Street - Tipping Street
Owned by City Surveyor
Capacity 200

1001. New Brown Street - Back Sugar Lane
Owned by City Surveyor
Capacity 175

1002. Alexandra Road South (Hartley College)
Owned by Hartley Victoria Ministerial Methodist College
Capacity 90

1003. 36 Dale Street
Owned by Pall Mall Property Company
Capacity 175

1005. 216 Bury New Road
Owned by F S Rhodes & Bathell Jones
Capacity 120

1009. 7A Nicholas Street
Owned by Heywood, Son & Hudson
Capacity 90

1010. Ainsworth Street (Ardwick)
Owned by F H Bamford
Capacity 200

1012. Bennett Street (St Benedict)
Owned by City Surveyor
Capacity 90

1013. 57 Brunswick Street
Owned by W & A Yates
Capacity 125

1014. 15 Cooper Street
Owned by City Surveyor
Capacity 180

1015. Crescent Street - Thurloe Street
Owned by Ministerial Training Committee
Capacity 170

1017. Heath Street, Newton Heath
Owned by J & R Philips & Co Ltd
Capacity 160

1020. 44A Market Street
Owned by M & F Westbrook
Capacity 140

1022. 22 Palatine Road
Owned by Manchester County Club
Capacity 100

1023. Rochdale Road (Victoria Avenue Cinema)
Owned by S Haling
Capacity 180

1024. Southgate (Kendals)
Owned by Kendal Milne & Co Ltd
Capacity 200 *SEE KENDALS CHAPTER*

1026. Wilmslow Road (Parrswood Court)
Owned by Parrswood Court
Capacity 200

1028. 125 Grosvenor Street
Owned by Manchester Citizens Club
Capacity 175

Victoria Avenue Cinema

1029. 171 Cheetham Hill Road
Owned by M & J Doherty
Capacity 100

1030. Oxford Street (Oxford Cinema)
Owned by J & F Emery Ltd
Capacity 120

1031. Oxford Street (Gaumont)
Owned by Gaumont Picture Corporation Ltd
Capacity 180

1032. Pottery Lane (Pineapple Hotel)
Owned by Openshaw Brewery
Capacity 200

1033. Church Street, Newton Heath
Owned by The Failsworth Industrial Co-op Society Ltd
Capacity 200

1034. Cheetham Hill Road (Crumpsall Library)
Owned by Libraries Committee
Capacity 170

1036. Milton Street
Owned by A Zuiligotti & Co
Capacity 70

1037. Oxford Road (University)
Owned by Vice Chancellor Victoria University
Capacity 150 - *SEE OVERLEAF*

1038. Grosvenor Square (Presbyterian Church
Owned by The Trustees Presbyterian Church
Capacity 200

1039. - (Cont School)
Owned by C W Provis & Sons
Capacity 200

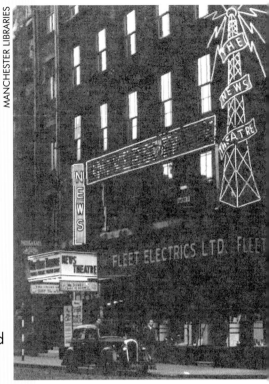

Oxford Cinema

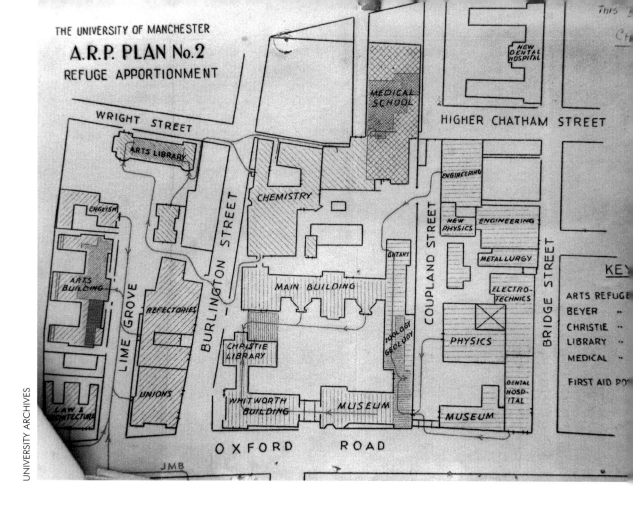

An unidentified University shelter

118

A.R.P. Control Room.
The University.
22nd. March 1941

PRIVATE AND CONFIDENTIAL.

Dear Vice-Chancellor,
          At Professor Thomson's suggestion I beg
to bring to your immediate notice the attached reports by Dr.
Sansome and myself on occurrences in the Medical Building about
midnight on the 22nd March.
          Early this morning I had a talk with Mrs.
O'Brian, the Shelter Warden, who revealed some very disquieting
alleged facts about student discipline in the Medical Building.
          She stated she would rather be without the assistance of
about half the student parties provided for the Medical Refuge.
She alleged that drunkenness was common, and that women were
brought into the University portion of the Building. She had
herself seen two women in immodest postures on mattresses in
Professor Raper's room in the presence of students, though with
no indication of actual immorality.
          There is difficulty in securing the rapid opening of
the street gates after a night siren warning.
          The occupants of the shelter are stated to have com-
mented adversely on the behaviour in public houses, and with
women, of persons stated by them to be University A.R.P. personnel.
          It seems only right that you should have this inform-
ation at the earliest opportunity. I am sending a copy of this
letter and the reports to the A.R.P. Committee.
                    Yours sincerely,
                                        J.C.S.Dickson.
                              Control Officer. 21.3.41.

Left: No doubt, students generally acted reponsibly during the war years, but this letter indicated perceived misconduct by some, as reported by the ARP warden

Below: Page from the University ARP handbook

The University ARP control room was in the telephone exchange. They did not receive air raid warnings by phone from central control at police headquarters, but had to rely on a porter at the main gates hearing the siren during the day, and wardens at night.

If the telephone lines at the Police Control Room in Moss Side were put out of action, provision was made, in 1941, for staff to transfer to the University.

The listed University refuges: Christie, which could accommodate 100, Library 130, Beyer 175, Arts 200, and Medical 175.

37.

CONTROL ROOM AND FIRE HEADQUARTERS.

17. Under mobilisation conditions it is intended that there shall normally be two Executive Officers on the premises, one in charge of the Control Room and one in charge of fire precautions.

Executive Officers "on duty".
(1) Location to be as far as possible continuously known to the Switchboard Operator, and suitable arrangements made in Departments etc. for the immediate forwarding of "Steam Caution" and other urgent messages.
(2) On receipt of "Steam Caution" immediately take charge in Control Room and Fire Headquarters respectively.

Executive Officers not "on duty" but on the premises on receipt of A.R. Warning:
Control Officers report to Control Room to act as reserve staff;
Fire Officers assist Fire Officer "on duty" as prearranged;
Assistant Control Officers carry out normal duties as Wardens etc. unless by previous arrangement they are required to assist in Control Room.

Shelters for 600 under Royal Exchange

Cellars 27ft below street level were converted into two large air-raid shelters. They accommodated 600, including the staff of 250 and 40 shops in the building.

The cellars ran around the outer edge of the building. The roofs were brick-arched, and although the cellars were strong they required timber supports.

The shelters were gas, blast, splinter and debris proof but they were not guaranteed to survive a direct hit. The cellars in the central basement were not used in case a bomb dropped through the glass dome 130ft down to the floor.

1041. Ashton Old Road (St Silas Church)
Owned by Parochial Church Council
Capacity 200

1042. Ashton Old Road (St Silas School)
Owned by Parochial Church Council
Capacity 175

1043. Cheetham Hill (Jews' Home)
Owned by The Trustees, Home for Aged Jews
Capacity 160

1044. 325 City Road
Owned by C Midgby Ltd
Capacity 200

1045. 2 Mount Street
Owned by Prudential Assurance Co Ltd
Capacity 200

1046. 7/9 Swann Street
Owned by Marshall, Gibbons & Co
Capacity 140

1047. Oldham Street (Hughes Stores)
Owned by Oldham Street Stores Ltd
Capacity 200

1051. Holt Town
Owned by Smith & Forest (Oils Ltd)
Capacity 200

1055. 49 Shudehill
Owned by J Sherlock & Sons Ltd
Capacity 200

1056. 97 Shudehill
Owned by G Hartley & Sons
Capacity 150

1057. 140 Stretford Road
Owned by E Riddick
Capacity 200

1058. 343 Stretford Road
Owned by S Kershaw
Capacity 110

1059. 58 Swann Street
Owned by T Spencer Andrew
Capacity 80

1062. 692 Ashton Old Road
Owned by Fred Fearnley Ltd
Capacity 130

1063. 929 Ashton Old Road
(St Barnabus Rectory)
Owned by Rev A Noble, St Barnabus Church
Capacity 75

1065. 25 John Dalton Street
Owned by W R Coe
Capacity 200

1066. 19 Mason Street
Owned by John Swift Ltd
Capacity 175

1067. Middleton Road (Ashdown)
Owned by Eli Fox
Capacity 150

1069. Travis Street (St Andrews)
Owned by Diocese of Manchester
Capacity 200

1070. 228 Upper Brook Street
Owned by W Curwen, Barrett & Sons
Capacity 175

Damage to Raid Shelters

The Manchester Emergency committee had before it a report by the City Surveyor of what he described as wilful damage in public shelters and communal-type shelters over a period of about four months. The report showed that 160 bunks and 24 partitions to chemical closets had been damaged, twenty windows in wardens' posts broken, blankets removed from 18 shelters, electrical fittings damaged and lamps stolen in 150 shelters, batten doors and frames broken, and concrete covers of emergency exits damaged, brick panels to emergency exits knocked out in seventy shelters, 150 forms damaged and 24 gully tops removed.

With regard to electrical equipment the City Surveyor reported that 650 lamps supplied by the Corporation Electricity Department had been stolen, and 500 supplied at the outset by the contractors either broken or stolen, 14 batteries were missing and 15 damaged, 144 lampholders, 44 switches, and 15 fuses were missing or damaged; about 75% of the hand lamps were missing, and there were 32 instances of damage to wiring.

The Town Clerk (Mr R H Adcock) said that in many cases the damage to the bunks had been done by deliberate slashing with a knife or other sharp instrument. It was presumed that the damage was done mostly by boys and mostly during the day.

Guardian February 1941

121

MANCHESTER LIBRARIES

Stretford Road Library

1072. 16 Withy Grove
Owned by J Battersby & Son
Capacity 150

1073. Stretford Road (Library)
Owned by Libraries Committee
Capacity 100

1075. 10/12 Alexandra Road South
Owned by Railton & Knowles
Capacity 175

1076. 133 Upper Brook Street
Owned by Miss P Hanratty, Mrs Olden
Capacity 400

1077. 5 Buckingham Crescent
Owned by Ellis & Sons
Capacity 140

1078. 27 Ardwick Green North
Owned by Ecclesiastical Commissioners
Capacity 150

1079. 49 Devonshire Street North
Owned by Miss Cameron
Capacity 50

1081. Albion Street, Miles Platting (St Lukes)
Owned by The Rector, St Lukes Rectory
Capacity 125

1082. 35 Hyde Road
Owned by E J Riley Ltd
Capacity 200

1083. Hyde Road (Methodist Chapel)
Owned by Mr Langman (Sec)
Capacity 100

1084. 153 Oxford Road
Owned by M Franks
Capacity 85

1085. 97/99 Oxford Road
Owned by John Alker & Co
Capacity 200

1086. Edge Street, Copperas Street
Owned by F Ryder for Exors of J Kelsall
Capacity 400

1087. Rochdale Road (Blackley Library)
Owned by Libraries Committee
Capacity 175

1089. 124 Withington Road
Owned by D B Robinson
Capacity 175

1090. 137 Lapwing Lane
Owned by J H Norris & Son
Capacity 150

1091. 121 Palatine Road
Owned by J H Norris & Son
Capacity 150

1092. 2/6 Major Street & 10 Aytoun Street
Owned by: J Ashworth & Sons Ltd,
& Manchester Mortgage & Investment Assurance
Capacity 470

1093. 31/35 Lloyd Street
Owned by W H Robinson & Co
Capacity 130

1094. 10/28 Tib Street
Owned by C & A Modes Ltd
Capacity 385

MANCHESTER LIBRARIES

Blackley Library

1095. 12 Swann Street
Owned by J Lea Axon
Capacity 120

1096. 219 Chester Road
Owned by Jos Sherlock & Son
Capacity 200

1097. 18 Long Millgate
Owned by Millgate Buildings
Capacity 200

1100. 69a Corporation Street
Owned by Exors of Wm Gilman
Capacity 180

1101. 1 Liverpool Road
Owned by R H & A Lord
Capacity 150

1103. 57/61 Market Street
Owned by G A Dunn & Co Ltd
Capacity 175

1104. 21 Marsden Square
Owned by Laban Spencer
Capacity 200

1105. 31 New Cannon Street
Owned by J R Bridgford & Son
Capacity 200

1106. 14 Todd Street (Pegg's Cafe)
Owned by J Sherlock & Son
Capacity 200

1107. 102/112 London Road
Owned by Earle Estates Ltd
Capacity 200

The Calico Printers Association on Oxford Street had eight basements to accommodate around 1,100 employees. The ceilings were strengthened with steel supports and the shelter entrances had an airlock with a further small sandbagged area. One basement was converted into a hospital with blankets and stretchers, and an emergency telephone systeminstalled. The company decided not to separate men and women in the shelters as this helped to reduce panic.

YOUR OWN OPINION . . .

Singing in Shelters

WHILE the sirens were sounding one night I went into a public air-raid shelter in Failsworth.

The warden advised us to sing, and we began singing all the latest dance hits. About 10 minutes later a police sergeant and a constable came in and told us that if we did not stop singing we would all have to leave.

I challenged the sergeant about his right to stop the singing, pointing out that the Home Secretary had made it clear that he desired people to be as cheerful as possible during raids. I was told by the sergeant that if I did not stop arguing I would have to leave. This I offered to do after informing the sergeant that he would take responsibility if I was killed or injured, and also pointed out that the matter would be mentioned to the Home Secretary.

I realise the police and air raid wardens have an unenviable task during the air raids, but I feel sure that stopping singing in shelters during raids is carrying officialdom a little too far.—**Freedom.**

❖ ❖ ❖

Animal Shelters

PROPOSALS are made by animal protection societies for the provision of refuges in London where owners can place

---

1109. 70 Oxford Street
Owned by J & J Shaw Ltd
Capacity 200

1110. Peter Street (Theatre Royal)
Owned by H D M Cinemas Ltd
Capacity 135

1112. 18 Mosley Street
Owned by Exors of A J Alexander
Capacity 150

1114. 49 Lower Mosley Street
Owned by Manchester Education Committee
Capacity 185

1115. 38 Oldham Street
Owned by J Lyons & Co Ltd
Capacity 175

1116. Barlow Road (Levenshulme Baths)
Owned by Manchester Corporation Baths
& Washhouses Committee
Capacity 40

'The warden advised us to sing, and we began singing all the latest dance hits. About ten minutes later a constable came in and told us if we did not stop singing we would all have to leave.'

The Drink Nuisance in Manchester

'A man and wife walked nearly two miles through the streets to reach their home because in the first shelter they entered there was a woman mad drunk, swearing and wanting to fight. In another shelter two men started fighting and the police had to be called. In a third shelter the conditions were, to quote an elderly woman who stayed in it a few minutes, 'perfectly beastly owing to the bad language and the number of men and women who were being sick'. And so I could go on for shelter after shelter; and in every case one hears of frightened children crying and women upset and hysterical.

I have since spoken to some forty ARP wardens, shelter wardens, auxiliary policemen, and similar persons, and in every case they told me that their chief difficulty was with drunken or half-drunken men and women. Yet on nights other than Saturday, and to a lesser degree Sunday, a shelter may contain two or three times as many people with no disorder or discomfort.'

Guardian September 1940

1117. Kenyon Lane (Moston Baths)
Owned by Manchester Corporation Baths & Washhouses Committee
Capacity 30

1118. 1 Broadway (Moston Baths)
Owned by Manchester Corporation Baths & Washhouses Committee
Capacity 50

1120. 200 Deansgate
Owned by Royal London Insurance Co
Capacity 150

1121. 82 High Street
Owned by Gaskell & Co (Bacup)
Capacity 200

1122. 84/6 Oldham Street
Owned by G J Fletcher
Capacity 200

1125. 38 Thomas Street
Owned by W H Carrington Ltd
Capacity 50

1126/7. 46/48 Thomas Street
Owned by J Wainwright & Sons
Capacity 185

1128. 75 Thomas Street
Owned by Trustees of L J Earle & Miney
Capacity 75

1129. 42 Raby Street, Moss Side
Owned by R H & A Lord
Capacity 175

1130. 127/133 Portland Street
Owned by Chepstow Street Development Ltd
Capacity 1300

1131. 95 Oldham Street
Owned by J Sears & Co Ltd
Capacity 100

1133. 91 Oldham Street
Owned by Town Tailors Ltd
Capacity 90

1134. 88 Oldham Street
Owned by J B Ellam & Son
Capacity 100

1135. 82 Oldham Street
Owned by Womersley & Tweedale
Capacity 125

1136. 45 Oxford Road
Owned by Driver, Jonas & Co
Capacity 100

1137. 112 Grosvenor Street
Owned by E H Street
Capacity 200

1140. 31 Tib Street
Owned by Tonkin & Ryder
Capacity 200

1145. 66/70 Market Street
Owned by (agents for owners) Isaac Neild, Son & Lees
Capacity 175

1147. Long Millgate (Phoenix Mill)
Owned by L M & S Railway Co
Capacity 175

1148. 37 Long Millgate
Owned by L M & S Railway Co
Capacity 115

'On Fridays, Saturdays and Sundays, numbers of drunken men and women as well as lads, stagger in and out of the shelters. Fights, quarrels, bad language, the deliberate damaging of sandbags are the result. Men and women stupefied with drink insist on leaving the shelters, often to collapse outside, sometimes injuring themselves so severely that police, ARP wardens, and shelter wardens have to render first aid in the open and expose themselves to unnecessary danger.'
SHELTER MARSHAL

Guardian September 1940

'...the conditions were, to quote an elderly woman who stayed in it a few minutes, 'perfectly beastly owing to the bad language and the number of men and women who were being sick'.

1149. 4 New Market Place
Owned by agent: A Whitworth
Capacity 150

1150. 76/80 Shudehill
Owned by the Markets Committee
Capacity 150

1152. Withy Grove & Dantzic Street
Owned by Withy Grove Stores Ltd
Capacity 115

1157. 102 Market Street
Owned by Henry Dodgson Ltd
Capacity 75

1158. Market Street - Palace Square
Owned by Isaac Nield, Son & Lees
Capacity 200

1159. 32/4 Market Street
Owned by J Lingard & Son
Capacity 100

1161. 74 Market Street
Owned by Isaac Nield Son & Lees
Capacity 90

1162. 25/29 Rochdale Road
Owned by F A Fitton, Wilson Smith & Martin
Capacity 175

1163. 1 Union Street
Owned by W H Sutton & Sons
Capacity 200

1164. 16 Bradshaw Street
Owned by CWS Ltd
Capacity 100

SHELTER "CLEAN-UP" PLANS

RELIGIOUS organisations in the Manchester area are completing their plans for helping to "clean up" public air raid shelters by dealing with drinking, gambling, swearing, and other offensive conduct.

"The matter is being dealt with," was all the Bishop of Manchester would say on the matter to-day, but it is understood that clergy and selected members of congregations in the various districts are being approached to take turns of duty around shelters in their particular area.

The town clerk's department has received letters from various religious organisations indicating a willingness to co-operate.

1167. 9/15 Market Street
Owned by Bowdens Ltd
Capacity 100

1169. 49 Swann Street
Owned by Markets Committee
Capacity 700

1171. Butler Street (Proposed flats)
No owner
Capacity 113

1172. Great Jackson Street (Proposed flats)
No owner
Capacity 109

1173. Every Street (Proposed flats)
No owner
Capacity 197

1174. Every Street - Russell Street
(Proposed flats)
No owner
Capacity 114

1176. Union Street (Proposed flats)
No owner
Capacity 450

1177. Gunson Street (Proposed flats)
No owner
Capacity 93

1178. 583/5 Stockport Road
Owned by Allendales Ltd
Capacity 140

1179. Hunts Bank (Victoria Station)
Owned by L M & S Railway
Capacity 400 - *SEE OVERLEAF*

Entertainment in Shelters

The Manchester Information Committee discussed the question of providing lectures and entertainments in public air-raid shelters, and expressed agreement with the Emergency Committee's view that the majority of the shelters are unsuitable for such activities.

Mr Edwin Furness, secretary of the committee, told a reporter that it was stated in the discussion that during the summer months, with their light nights, there would be no need to provide against 'shelter boredom'.

'If the need for shelter life continues next winter' he added, 'the committee proposes to discuss with the Emergency Committee the organisation of lectures and entertainments in selected shelters subject to the needs and desires of the shelter users themselves'.

Guardian April 1941

1180. Arch 90 - Hewitt Street
Owned by L N & E Railway
Capacity 200

1181. Arch - London Road/ Store Street
Owned by L M & S Railway
Capacity 100

1182. Arch 52 (New Wakefield Street)
Owned by L M & S Railway
Capacity 320

1183. Arch 136 - London Road Station
Owned by L M & S Railway
Capacity 600

Victoria Station shelter

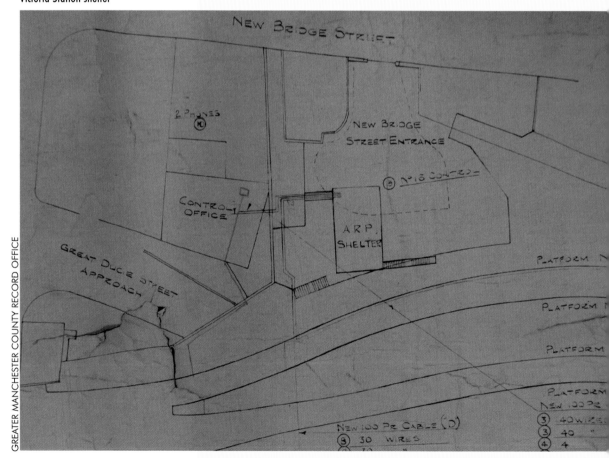

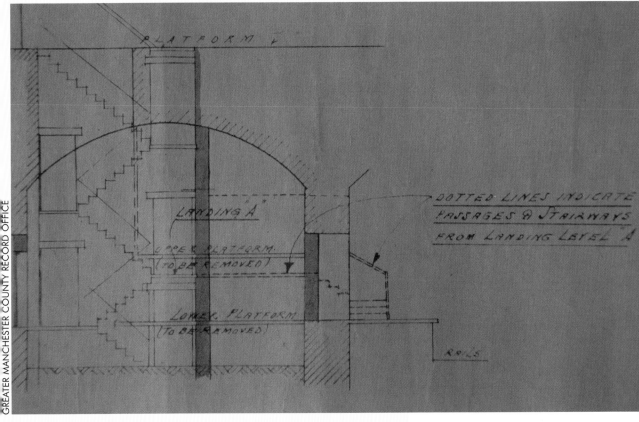

Piccadilly Station shelter

1184. Arch Fairfield Street (London Road Station)
Owned by L M & S Railway
Capacity 575

1185. 7 Spring Gardens
Ownership and capacity - not stated

Canal Arm, Manchester & Salford Junction Canal
(Grape Street)
Owned by Manchester Ship Canal Co
Capacity 1368 - *SEE MANCHESTER & SALFORD JUNCTION CANAL CHAPTER*

Victoria Arches (Great Ducie Street)
Owned by Manchester Corporation
Capacity 1619 - *SEE VICTORIA ARCHES CHAPTER*

Victoria Arches

This the story of one of Manchester's biggest road improvement schemes - the creation of an important new entrance to the town. It was constructed over ground sloping down from the Cathedral to the river Irwell and supported by arches. This arched space has been a source of curiosity. People have suggested there were businesses, roadways and even shops down there. Looking back over the history of this road and its under-space we find stories of bravery, tragedy, innovation and a place in which crowds have gathered to celebrate, or to witness the effects of storms and other disasters. Later, it was to become a place of refuge for many during WW2.

ROAD WIDENING

Estimates had been drawn up in 1827 for creating an improved road link between Bury New Road and Hunts Bank. It was later claimed in a letter to the Guardian that the arched structure had been first suggested by the engineer Isambard Kingdom Brunel whose opinion had been sought by the planning authority of those times - the Commissioners. The stretch of road at Hunts Bank had the reputation of being particularly dangerous, and this was highlighted by Thomas Pintoff at the Police Commissioners meeting in 1832, urging that the road should be improved as a matter of urgency after one of his friends had met with a serious accident and two others had been in danger.

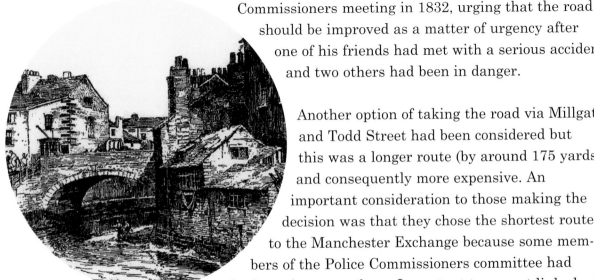

Old bridge over the Irk

Another option of taking the road via Millgate and Todd Street had been considered but this was a longer route (by around 175 yards), and consequently more expensive. An important consideration to those making the decision was that they chose the shortest route to the Manchester Exchange because some members of the Police Commissioners committee had business interests there. Important transport links had already been completed. A new bridge over the Irk at its junction with the Irwell had been built in 1826 and Ducie Street opened 19 October 1831. Bury New Road between Hunts Bank and the Turnpike at Pilkington opened on 19 December 1833.

On 3 March 1832, plans were announced to widen the road from Hunts Bank bridge to the yard of the Collegiate Church. This would involve the purchase and demolition of property along its route. It was reported in September 1832 that enquiries had been made to purchase property to build the road but the land owners'

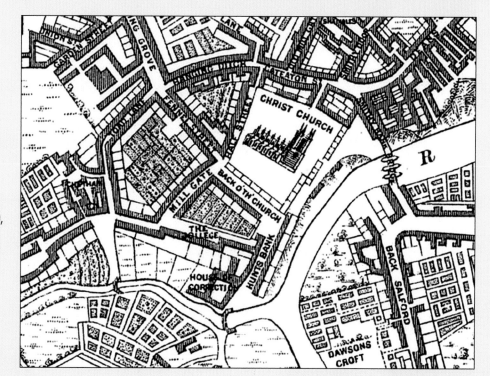

Right: Manchester in 1751. Note the House of Correction by the bridge at Hunts Bank

Below: An impression of Manchester around 1760, showing the cluster of buildings at Hunts Bank which later became the site of the new road into the city.

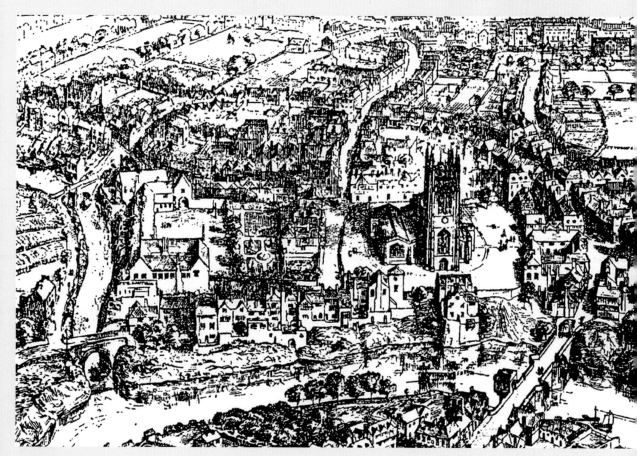

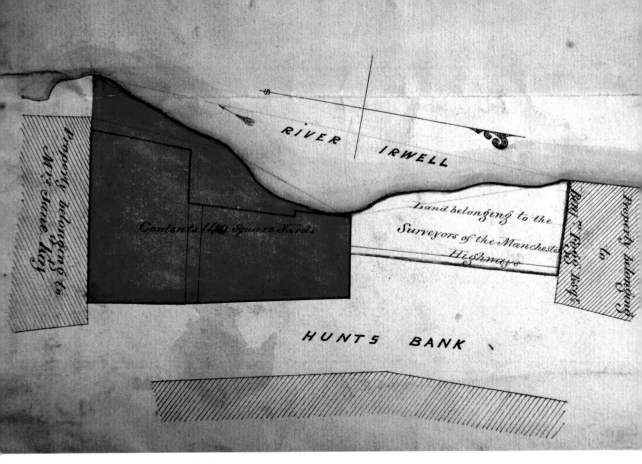

RIVER IRWELL

Contents 140 Square Yards

Land belonging to the Surveyors of the Manchester Highways

HUNTS BANK

MANCHESTER COUNCIL LEGAL RECORDS

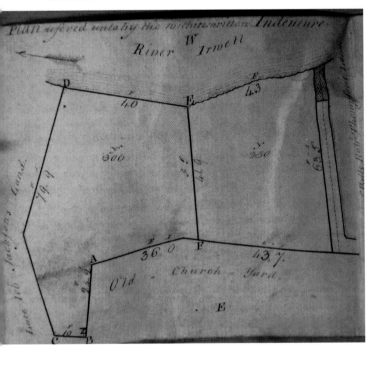

River W. Irwell

Plan referred unto by the within written Indenture

Old - Church - Yard.

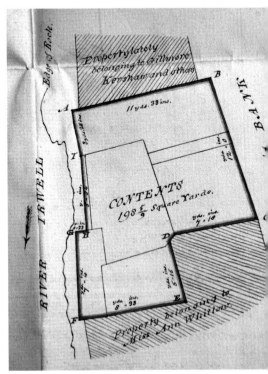

RIVER IRWELL

Property lately belonging to Gillmore Kershaw and others

CONTENTS 198⅘ Square Yards.

Property belonging to Miss Ann Whitton.

BANK

'extravagant' valuations had prevented further progress. The construction of the more direct route passing in front of the Cathedral, as recommended by the Improvements Committee on 25 November, was passed at a meeting of the Police Commissioners on 1 December 1832. This included the purchase of land on the northerly side of Old Bridge Street from the trustees of the late Mr Stelfox to improve the approach to the road and the proposed new bridge into Salford. The cost of the 655 square yards was £1650.

Work commenced on the road improvement in 1833, under the direction of the contractor and manager of the works Thomas Taylor, from Bolton. There was criticism that profits from Manchester's gas supply were being used on widening Hunts Bank.

At the meeting of the Commissioners in April 1833 it was agreed to purchase land owned by John Harrison, and Messrs Barratt and Turner, (trustees for Mrs Jane Kay), with the possibility of taking the issue before an independent jury for a final decision on land and property valuation. The need for change was emphasised, because the narrowness of the road through Hunts Bank meant there was not enough room for two carriages to pass each other, and a footpath which was less than 2ft wide. Mr Pintoff commented it was possibly the most dangerous place in Manchester to pass through. During the race meetings at Kersal Moor there were particular problems with the crowds passing along the narrow road at Hunts Bank and special constables had to be deployed.

Opposite : Agreements between land owners and the Commissioners to purchase land for the arched roadway.

Below: The new road would bring an improved road connection to the Kersal Moor race meetings.

On 5 July 1833, the Improvement Committee advertised for a contractor to build the river wall by Hunts Bank Bridge, remove the remains of the soapery belonging to Fogg Birch and Hampson, and to demolish two cottages. The soapery and other buildings had slipped into the Irwell in July 1814 with the loss of three lives.

In the fifth annual report of the Improvements Committee, it stated that arrangements with Lord Ducie, Harrison and others, Fogg, Kershaw and others had been made for the purchase of property extending from beyond Hunts Bank Bridge to the raised terrace near the Cathedral Steps. Also, work was under way on the river wall from the bridge at Hunts Bank down to the end of the river by the old soapery. The cost of this part of the improvement was estimated at £4595, of which £2925 had already been paid.

ACCIDENTS

The first reported mishap during construction occurred when heavy rain and flooding swept away some of the

Below: The Irk by Chetham's where the rescued boy fell in and was swept under the bridge and into the Irwell. This section of the river was culverted in 1845.

MANCHESTER LIBRARIES

Above: The completed river wall c1850

supports and planking from the site as far as New Bailey
Bridge on 7 September 1833, causing work on the project
to be briefly halted. During a storm on 19 July 1834 a
four year old boy slipped into the swollen waters of the
river Irk near the back of Chethams College and he was
carried under the Hunts Bank bridge and into the new
workings on the river Irwell. The incident was seen by
John Quinn (better known by his nickname 'Irish Jack'),
one of the labourers working on the road improvement,
who bravely dived into the Irwell and managed to grab
the hair of the struggling child as he slipped under the
water and bring him to safety. After medical attention
the boy soon recovered from his ordeal.

By 30 August 1834 the Improvement Committee reported
good progress had been made on the bridge and wall.
A large portion had been built and it was optimistically
hoped that the remainder of the carriage road and foot-

path would be completed and in use by the end of that year. They were working to the plans provided by the Police Commission surveyor George Shorland, and the Committee dismissed criticism that the river wall encroached the boundary of the Irwell.

The contract for the iron railings along 124 yards of the wall was published 15 November 1834. One year later legal provisions for lighting and sewering the improvement were announced. The cost of the Hunts Bank Improvement between 1834 and 1839 was £1929. In November 1835 application was made by the Commissioners for an Act of Parliament for the new road between Hunts Bank and Cateaton Street, along with other street improvements in the centre of Manchester.

William Royle, a labourer on the scheme, died on 20 May 1835 after being crushed by a three-ton stone, as it was being manoeuvred into the foundations of the river wall. He had only started work there at noon of that day. Mr Taylor, the contractor, and two other labourers who were also close to the incident managed to avoid serious injury.

Work was under way to extend the river wall by July 1835 for the road described as an 'important and valuable' route between Strangeways and Cateaton Street, and there was optimism that it would be completed before the approach of winter. Since the last report, premises occupied and belonging to Mallieu and Lees near the old bridge, had been purchased, along with land from Barrett and Harrison.

WALL COLLAPSE

There was a major setback to the scheme in 1836 when part of the new river wall collapsed. A section by the Black Moor's Head inn fell into the river with such force that it severely damaged the three-storey high premises of William Collier and Co, fustian shearers and machine makers, on the opposite bank about forty yards away.

The danger was first noted by workmen at Hunts Bank arriving at first light on Saturday 29th January. A 100ft length of the 30-ft high wall had begun to separate from the rock and the ground was rapidly breaking up. Mr Shorland, the site surveyor for the Commissioners was immediately notified, but nothing could be done to stop the impending disaster. At 8.25am the wall and all the infill earth, with a combined estimated weight of 1500 tons, crashed down. The violence of the force of the fall exposed the river bed, and for a few moments the huge wall of spray thrown up obscured what had happened to the building belonging to Colliers', on the Salford side of the river. When the spray subsided, the horrified spectators could see that there were three large holes in the facing wall, and a large portion of the roof had gone. It was likened to the buildings being hit by a broad-side from a 'man of war'. The machinery and the goods in the building were buried under tons of debris and they feared for the safety of the factory workers. Fortunately, the employees had gone for breakfast at the time of the wall collapse.

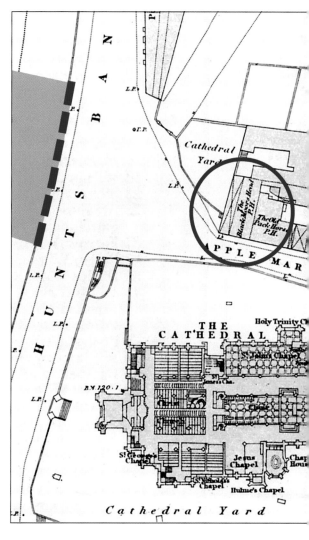

The Blackmoor's Head Inn and the probable site of the wall collapse

The accident had been caused by a burst water pipe to the Black Moor's Head and other demolished buildings in the vicinity. It had been noticed the previous Wednesday, but it took until the following day for the pipe to be mended. The site surveyor was not informed about the problem which was worsening. By that time around 100 tons of water had already seeped into the loose earth

Victoria Arches c1909 from
the Salford side of the Irwell

behind the wall and, unknown to the workmen, the semi-fluid mass was causing major problems. On the following day, Friday, no-one worked on site because of the bad weather. If they had, they would have seen the worsening situation described in one newspaper as 'the approaching mischief' and taken steps to prevent it.

The incident and its aftermath drew many people to view the damage. This was a great opportunity for pickpockets to mingle with the crowds. Some of the criminals were spotted and beaten up by members of the public and one thief was taken into custody and sentenced to a months hard labour. The river wall cost £300 to repair, and the Commissioners paid out a total of £775 in compensation for damage on the opposite side of the Irwell caused by the collapse, including £300 to Collier and Company's machine shop. The premises of Collier's seemed to be vulnerable, because they suffered further damage in 1837 after heavy flooding, and then in April 1844 when the machine shop collapsed into the river. Fortunately there were no injuries in any of the incidents, but the last collapse cost the owner around £500 to replace damaged machinery.

In April 1836 agreement had still be reached for compensation to be given to Horatio Skerritt and William Cook for their premises. By September 1836 it was reported that £4360 had been paid for land owned and occupied by Mallalieu and Lees. On the twenty-six yards of roadway near Hunts Bank bridge, the Flying Horse tavern had been built at a cost of £10. Property had been purchased in Old Bridge Street from Mr Stevenson to open out the southern end of the new road.

ROAD PROGRESS

The following year progress was reported on the new road through Hunts Bank and Smithy Door, including the demolition of the buildings on the Mallalieu and Lees land. It was announced that four of the arches below the road were ready for occupation. Also, contracts had been agreed for the extension of the river wall and railings up to the site of the proposed new bridge to Salford. The road was being extended to Cateaton Street, and property acquired to widen Smithy Door.

Some of the construction materials for the project were stored in the collegiate church yard. A man was arrested in the vicinity by the police in the early hours of the morning in August 1837 after stealing a plank from the churchyard, and sentenced to 14 days' hard labour.

By September 1837 the section of the new road at Hunts Bank was ready to be paved and flagged to prevent surface water seeping into the unfinished arches

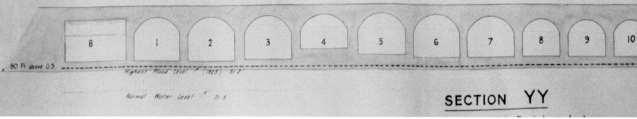

further along. However, the work was not implemented for some time because in the Highways minutes, August 1841, there was the directive 'That Hunts Bank be paved with Bugsworth sets'.

The river wall damaged in January in 1836 had not been repaired, and in December 1837 the Improvement Committee received a letter from the Trustees of the Grammar School urging them to take action. Possibly the delay in the paving and flagging was due to the rebuilding of the river wall.

During a heavy storm on the morning of Friday 6 October 1837 William Mawkes was passing the road workings by the Cathedral Church Yard on his way to work. He found his normal route was blocked by a horse and cart and as he passed on the other side he got too close to the iron tyre of the cart wheel and was struck by lightning. He fell some way down the slope into the Arches onto loose stones and bricks. He was taken back to his lodgings nearby in Strangeways where he regained consciousness. He had bad bruising from his fall and severe shock.

It was exceptionally cold in March 1838 with the River Irwell partially freezing over at Hunts Bank. At a council meeting on the 16th, it was claimed that the new street had cost between £60,000 and £100,000.

A workman was killed on 9 April 1838 as the foundations dug to a depth of 16ft for an arch had collapsed on top of

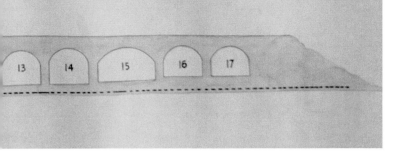

Sectional drawing of the Arches from the war-time shelter plan

him. Ten minutes earlier, four workmen had come across water seeping into sand and, although they realised this was dangerous, they continued to work. The deceased had been trying to escape up a ladder when falling earth buried him. Rescuers reached his body after forty-five minutes.

UNOFFICIAL OPENING

The new road through Hunts Bank unofficially opened on Saturday morning 9 May 1838 with walkers and the first equestrian - Mr Milne on his pony - making their way over bricks and other materials from the road construction, which still had to be cleared. But all was was made ready for the official opening the week before Whit (5 June) in readiness for the huge influx of carriages, horse-riders and pedestrians going to the four day race festival at Kersal Moor. The new road would cut about two hundred yards off the journey for carriages into Manchester. Also, because it was spacious and mostly straight, it made journeys much safer.

Smithy Door was still being paved, and the new river wall could not be completed until it linked up to the Victoria bridge, which was under construction. By the September, all the arches were completed.

On Wednesday 28th June, Manchester and Salford celebrated the accession of Queen Victoria. There was a horse-drawn procession of civic and church dignitaries, huge crowds waved flags, there were flags on many build-

An equestrian reader wrote to the Guardian in May 1838:

'The Public are now beginning to enjoy the advantage of the opening to the New Bury Road, at Hunts Bank. Allow me to suggest the great additional convenience which would arise to a large class of persons, if the proper authorities would mac-adamize that portion of the road between the Old Church and Strangeways turnpike. The mac-adamization need not be the whole width of the road, but might be the centre portion only; and nothing, perhaps, after the opening at Hunts Bank itself, would so greatly facilitate communication with Broughton and Prestwich.'

ing, and church bells rang. As the clocks on churches struck twelve o'clock, the artillery who had stationed themselves on the new road at Hunts Bank, and with their guns pointing up river, fired a twenty one gun salute. This was followed by the playing of the national anthem by the bands of the cavalry and infantry in St Ann's Square, to the great cheers of the crowds. The boroughreeve of Manchester, John Hyde, then read out the proclamation to Queen Victoria in the Square, which was lined by the Irish Dragoon Guards cavalry. The crowd gave a hearty three cheers and waved hats, handkerchiefs, bonnets, scarves, and the military their sabres. The same ceremony was repeated in Salford at the Town Hall, in Chapel Street at Trinity Chapel, and at Greengate. The two carriage party of dignitaries then returned to Manchester for a fourth gun salute, again from the new road at Hunts Bank, and a proclamation outside the Town Hall on King Street. The celebrations on a warm and sunny day had lasted three hours and, in spite of the large crowds, had taken place without incident.

ANVIL SALUTE

When the new Victoria Bridge opened on 22 June 1839, large crowds gathered in the fine weather, and it was reported that the new road along Hunts Bank was lined with many spectators. We have the first indication of the businesses in the Arches because employees from one of the companies made their own special contribution to the proceedings. Workmen from the forges brought out six large anvils near to the foreshore of the bridge. They arranged them like a battery of cannons and filled a hollow in the anvils with gunpowder from which they set off several rounds of loud reports.

Victoria Terrace was completed August 1839, and the road improvement was officially completed with the open-

146

Guardian, October 1839

ing of Victoria Street on September 21. The Improvement Committee in their report the following year were able to state, with some satisfaction *'This street is now open ... affording commodious and direct communication from the centre of town to Salford and to the Bury New Road, greatly relieving the adjacent, narrow and crowded thoroughfares, as well as being conducive to the health of the town by the admission of a current of air into a previously confined locality'.*

In October 1839, the arched vaults under Victoria Terrace were advertised as being suitable for wine merchants, printers and machine makers.

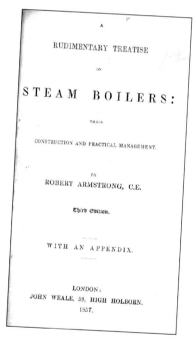

A
RUDIMENTARY TREATISE
ON
STEAM BOILERS:
THEIR
CONSTRUCTION AND PRACTICAL MANAGEMENT.

BY
ROBERT ARMSTRONG, C.E.

Third Edition.

WITH AN APPENDIX.

LONDON:
JOHN WEALE, 59, HIGH HOLBORN.
1857.

ROBERT ARMSTRONG

Robert Armstrong, a civil engineer, was one of the earliest tenants. By October of 1840 he was trading at the Arches and manufacturing Scott's patent boiler cleaners. Two years before, his office address had been 1 Withington Street, Pendlebury, where he was also supplying Cheetham's improvements to steam engines and furnaces. In 1830 his business address was at 4 Norfolk Street, Manchester, selling and manufacturing boiler apparatus. In a court case at New Bailey, Manchester in 1833 he was called

VICTORIA ARCHES.—R. ARMSTRONG, Civil and Mechanical Engineer, and Manufacturer of SCOTT'S PATENT BOILER CLEANERS, has REMOVED his BUSINESS to the above convenient premises, near the Victoria Bridge. The above apparatus can now be made complete for any kind of land boiler, at from £8 to £12 each, exclusive of fixing, &c. which varies from £2 to £5, according to distance and other circumstances. R. A. continues, as usual, to advise parties on the construction and setting up of boilers, and steam-engine works generally. Factory engines *indicated* and correctly calculated, and the power required to work any given machinery also estimated by various other methods.

Plate 3.

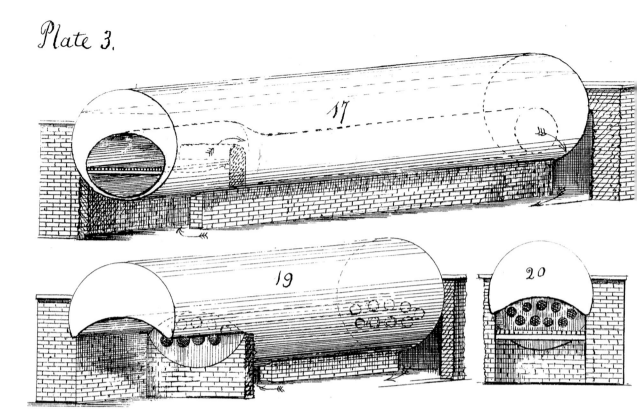

Boilers and brickwork drawings from 'A Practical Essay on Steam Engine Boilers' by Robert Armstrong

as an expert witness to give his opinion in a case regarding excessive smoke coming from the chimney of a cotton spinner.

Armstrong wrote several books on the subject of improving the efficiency of chimneys and steam engine boilers between 1837 and 1842 which received praise from the 'Civil Engineer and Architect's Journal'. John Bourne, who provided notes to Armstrong's 1856 edition of his book on boiler engineering, commented in his introduction that Armstrong 'had a more extended experience, and possesses probably a more accurate acquaintance with boilers than any other person now living ...'. The third edition of his treatise on the construction and management of steam boilers came out in 1857. By December 1848 Armstrong had vacated the Arches, and his patented boiler-cleaning apparatus was being manufactured by William Oxley at his Bale Street Works, off Lower Mosley Street. Oxley was continuing to supply Armstrong's boilers around 1855.

London move

Armstrong moved to London to earn his living as a consulting engineer, boiler and furnace architect and surveyor of steam engines and other machinery. He was living at 289 Winchester Street, London in 1851. Writing from 16 Anderson's Buildings, City Road, London, in 1854, he was endorsing the system for efficient boilers produced by Green's Phoenix Works in Wakefield. The preface of the revised edition of his book in 1856 was written at Fenchurch Street, London. The 1861 Census lists him as a civil engineer and living with his wife and two children in East Ham.

Poverty

Armstrong's circumstances later changed for the worse and he died in 1868, at the age of seventy three, in poverty in his native Durham near Stockton. His wife, Maria, died soon afterwards leaving their children destitute. 'The Engineer' journal described Anderson's life as without reproach, and commented on the excellence of his writings on steam boilers. Also, that he had been well-known in Manchester as a skilful boiler engineer and had worked under the the patronage of the Fairburn engineering company. The journal's readers were invited to contribute to a fund to pay off the funeral costs and other small debts.

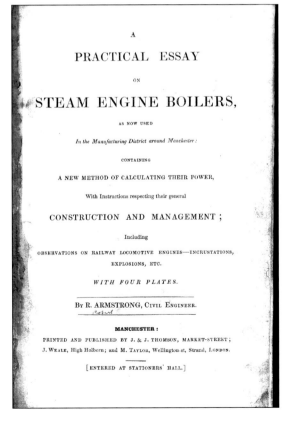

A

PRACTICAL ESSAY

ON

STEAM ENGINE BOILERS,

AS NOW USED

In the Manufacturing District around Manchester:

CONTAINING

A NEW METHOD OF CALCULATING THEIR POWER,

With Instructions respecting their general

CONSTRUCTION AND MANAGEMENT ;

Including

OBSERVATIONS ON RAILWAY LOCOMOTIVE ENGINES—INCRUSTATIONS, EXPLOSIONS, ETC.

WITH FOUR PLATES.

BY R. ARMSTRONG, CIVIL ENGINEER.

MANCHESTER :

PRINTED AND PUBLISHED BY J. & J. THOMSON, MARKET-STREET ;
J. WEALE, High Holborn ; and M. TAYLOR, Wellington-st, Strand, LONDON.

[ENTERED AT STATIONERS' HALL.]

NEW ARCHES ENTRANCE

Investigations began in April 1840 to adjust the road level of Cateaton Street and also the sloping entrance into the Arches. In 1842, the expiration of the lease held by the Von Blucher public house on Cateaton Street enabled the property to be purchased and then taken down to improve the line of the street.

By December 25 1843, three arches were let to Pasco Grenfell, copper merchants, at an annual rent of £40, paid quarterly. On April 1844, work began on the improvement of the corner of Cateaton Street and the new Hunts Bank Road. The Blucher spirit vaults had been dismantled and the building materials auctioned, in order to create a curved corner. The slope of the southern cartway entrance into Victoria Arches was situated here. It was not until 1845 that the improvement was completed on Cateaton St/Victoria Terrace. The cartway into Victoria Arches was closed, with the agreement of the tenants, and substituted with steps. A new cartway entrance was made at the other end of the Arches at Fennel Street. This entrance is shown on the Ordnance Survey map which was surveyed in 1849.

Gated entrance to the Arches at Fennel Street

VICTORIA ARCHES.

To the EDITOR of the MANCHESTER GUARDIAN.

Sir,—Will you allow me, through your paper, to complain of the gross neglect of the town in allowing the obstructions of the passages of these arches to remain in the disgraceful state in which they are day after day, to the serious inconvenience of persons going there on business. I this morning met with an accident through falling over a cask. I think the town authorities should immediately cause to be removed the old iron, casks, gates, &c. with which the passages are at present stopped up. — I am, sir, your obedient servant,   JOHN MORRIS.
Deansgate, July 21st, 1847.

A correspondent to the Guardian in July 1847 complained about the 'gross neglect' of the town authorities over the 'disgraceful state' of the passage to the arches. John Morris had been injured there while visiting on business after falling over a cask but had recovered sufficiently, later that day, to write a letter to the Guardian urging the authorities to order the removal of the iron work, casks,

and gates that cluttered the cartway. The letter writer,
John Morris was presumably the beer retailer listed at
Tickle Street off Deansgate in a trade directory for 1847.

THE RICHARDSON LIFEBOAT

On Thursday 15 January 1852 large cheering crowds
gathered to witness the unusual sight of a lifeboat being
launched in Manchester. The craft, built to a specification
and scale never seen before, was lowered by pulleys with
some difficulty from the Arches into the river in the
fading light of the afternoon. It had taken six months to
construct 'Challenger' at the workshops of William Lees
(formerly Lees and Lister) and was manned by a crew
of ten and a steersman. With its inventors also on board,
the tubular boat was soon on her way up the Irwell
to take part in sea trials from Liverpool.

The Richardson lifeboat

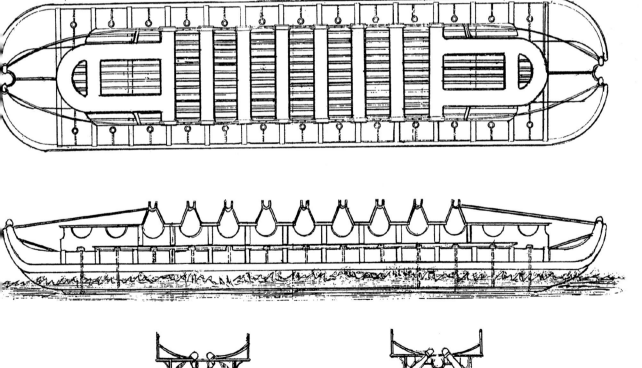

The boat was the brain-child of Henry Richardson, assisted by his son Henry Thomas and was the latest design in their attempt to produce a new, safer lifeboat. Over the years there had been many sea tragedies and a competition had been organised to make the work of lifeboatmen safer. The Richardson prototype was one of 360 selected by the Admiralty to compete for the Duke of Northumberland Prize. From these entrants, a model of Richardson's boat was amongst fifty to be displayed at the Great Exhibition. However, the Northumberland prize went to James Beeching for his self-righting lifeboat but the result was contested by the Richardsons. They had some justification to be aggrieved, because Beeching's boat had capsized during trials at Caernarfon in 1852 and had to be dragged back to the shore. The idea of double-hulled boats originated in the Far East centuries ago and they were first seen in this country in the late seventeenth century. The first significant lifeboat using two wood-framed cylinders was built in 1813.

The launch of the 'Challenger' in Manchester was an attempt to demonstrate the capabilities of their revolutionary new boat which basically consisted of two 40ft watertight iron tubes, two and a half ft in diameter and fitted 3ft apart, with the ends tapered and curved to join at the head and stern. The tubes were linked to iron arches which connected with a battened frame to support a platform for the rowers, seated in two rows, and crew. Along the outside of the tubes was a cork fender which people in the water could hold on to. The boat carried two four-sided 'lug' main sails, and a jib sail. Because of its unusual design, newspaper reporters debated whether it should be described as a boat or a raft.

It would have been a rather exposed, uncomfortable position for the crew, but relatively safe. The Richardsons

It would have been a rather exposed, uncomfortable position for the crew, but relatively safe.

claimed the boat could not sink, nor be swamped or water-logged. In tests they proved that when sixty people jumped onto it at the same time, as they would have done during an emergency, it stayed upright. It was thought it could be used in Arctic regions or a coastal situation.

Richardson had first experimented with the idea between 1830 and 1831 when he had four boats of increasing size built at Weymouth and then tried out on Lake Bala in Wales close to where he lived. By 1850 a Richardson boat was already in operation at Douglas in the Isle of Man, and the following year a patent for the tubular construction was taken out. This was probably built at the Arches, as the press report for the launch of 'Challenger' stated that previous smaller Richardson boats came from here.

The ten rowers were volunteers from the Welsh Fusiliers who wanted to support the Richardsons, who were both

In tests they proved that when sixty people jumped onto it at the same time, as they would have done during an emergency, it stayed upright.

officers in the Dragoon Guards. Henry, senior, was a retired lieutenant, and his son was quartered in Manchester.

Sabotage

After an overnight stay at Lymm, the boat journeyed to Liverpool via Runcorn. During the trials at Liverpool deficiencies in performance were experienced, and the Manchester boat-makers were summoned. It was found that the boat had been seemingly sabotaged on the starboard side with evidence of eighteen attempts to perforate the sides of the tube with a sharp instrument. Although a reward of fifty guineas was offered, the perpetrators were never discovered. At this point the Richardsons installed an iron rudder rather than steer with an oar, and also fitted 'Challenger' with sails and a mast.

Challenge

Once repairs were completed, the Richardsons issued a challenge to any life-boat owner to go through the same extensive trials as their boat. They waited four months in Liverpool before the owners of the Prize boat, the only one who agreed to take part, insisted that the trials should be at Ramsgate. The 'Challenger' crew set sail, safely negotiating the difficult waters of the Menai Straits and then on through storms along the Welsh coast. At several places where it was tested, 'Challenger' was praised for its strength and stability as it made its way through bad weather. At Barmouth it was described as the most perfect life-boat ever seen.

Masks

Whenever the boat passed near to the coastline or other boats, the crew put on masks of animals and demons to put off unwanted conversation and contact with other crews. The masks were also useful in providing protection from the effects of the sea-spray and wind. The journey ended at Ramsgate on 22 June for the intended head-to-

Whenever the boat passed near to the coastline or other boats, the crew put on masks of animals and demons to put off unwanted conversation and contact with other crews.

head trials. However, the winning boat had been acquired in the meantime by new owners, who, perhaps fearing the worst, refused to allow it to go through the trial because the builders would not guarantee to repair any damage incurred. When it was clear that trials were not going to take place, 'Challenger' journeyed to Woolwich in order that the Duke of Northumberland could see the boat for himself. The meeting with the Duke was very brief because he had been delayed by previous duties and could not stay to watch 'Challenger' in action.

The Richardson tubular lifeboat 'Rescue', launched at New Brighton in 1863

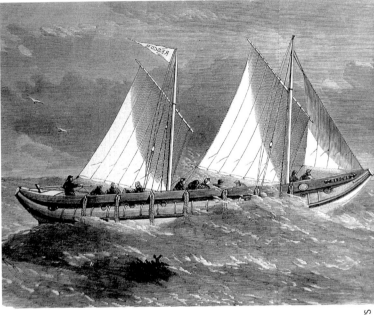

After taking part in a brief set of rowing trials, 'Challenger' was moored at Lambeth and the Richardsons and crew returned home. They seemed to be resigned to the fact that their lifeboat was not going to be generally accepted. However in 1853 'Challenger' was bought by the Portuguese government for service at Oporto.

Arches launch

A smaller version, about half the length of 'Challenger', to be used on board African mail boats was built at Laird's boatyard, Birkenhead and launched from Lees's in the Arches into the Irwell in May 1854. From 1856 a Richardson tubular lifeboat 'Morgan' was used at Rhyl, North Wales and helped save 32 lives in eight incidents. 'Rescue', a Richardson life-boat, was used at New Brighton from 1863. Tubular boats continued to be used at New Brighton and Rhyl, including the 'Henry Richardson' at the New Brighton station from 1888 to 1898. The last tubular life-boat was the 'Caroline Richardson II' based at Rhyl between 1897 and 1939.

Henry Richardson, who was also deputy lieutenant for Merionethshire and a magistrate, died aged 70 at Rhiwaedog Llanfor Bala in 1861. The cause of death was stated as 'Mortification of Leg' and 'Morbus Brightii'. His son died in 1878 and left £500 towards the establishment of a life-boat station at Pwllheli, which opened in 1890.

155

ARCHES HOIST ACCIDENT

In July 1859, two men were killed in a hoist accident at the Arches. They were employees of Cameron and Company, ale and porter merchants, agents for brewers Worthington and Robinson of Burton-upon-Trent. The company occupied some of the arches and had reached agreement with Manchester Corporation to rent another arch if an office was built onto the river wall by the Victoria Bridge. The premises, with stairs leading down to the Arches, were used afterwards by Thomas Cook and Sons. The two men had been using the hoist next to the office to lower six barrels of ale to the arch, when it stuck and a crowbar was used to force the mechanism. This caused chains to snap and fixing bolts to come out, and the two victims were hurled 30ft into the river with the falling barrels, hitting the wall of the Arches as they fell. One was instantly killed as he collided with an ironwork frame, and the other survived the fall and tried to swim to safety but disappeared further upstream.

Above: Hoist accident site
Below: The offices originally built for Cameron and Company

Afterwards, it became clear that the construction of the hoist was not complete, with the extra chains and pulleys required, and that it had not had a safety check by the Corporation. It also transpired that the hoist had been unofficially used for the previous two weeks to bring barrels out of the store on the instructions of Mr Cameron. Prior to the incident, four barrels had been safely lowered, which prompted the much bigger load, with tragic consequences.

SALFORD LOCAL STUDIES LIBRARY

ATTEMPTED ROBBERY

In December 1860 there had been several attempts
to rob a jeweller's shop by entering through the Arches.
Thomas Hammond, a jewellery, watch and clock maker
had premises on Victoria Terrace, immediately above the
Arches. There had been a cartway into the underground
premises but this had been converted into steps. This
area could still be accessed via the later gated entrance
to the cartway on the corner of Fennel Street and
Victoria Street by the Cathedral. The thieves tried to
force a way, from below, through the floor of his shop
but the proprietor had reinforced it with thick iron plates.
Mr Hammond and family who also lived on the premises
had not heard anything during the night. He only
discovered evidence of the attempted break-in when he
came into the Arches, the following morning, to check
on his favourite dog and pups which he kept down there.

In a letter to the Guardian in 1900, a correspondent wrote about a closed-off door he had been shown in the cellars of the Hanging Bridge pub. He was informed by the landlord that it opened into an underground passage which he claimed led under the river Irwell to Ordsal Hall. A previous tenant who had been down but had turned back because of the bad smells.

LIGHTNING STRIKE

In July 1871, during a thunderstorm,
the chimney belonging to the businesses in the Arches was struck by lightning. Coping stones fell onto the pavement and also caused damage to the
roof of a nearby photographic business,
and another stone narrowly missed
a passing cab. Later the chimney was
found to be unstable and had to be
taken down. The Courier newspaper
reporter described the dramatic event:
*'... in the morning continuous showers
of rain fell, and at about three o'clock
in the afternoon a very heavy shower
preceded a fearfully vivid flash of lightning and a peal of thunder which lasted for several seconds. At about half past three o'clock these were succeeded*

The Arches chimney next
to the Cathedral c1851

157

by an equally vivid flash of lightning and a thunderbolt which broke with a terrific crash over the city. Many persons in the immediate neighbourhood of Market Street and Victoria Street, who had taken shelter from the heavy downfall of rain were greatly alarmed by the occurrence,

many of the horses in the streets plunged violently, and the traffic in the streets for a few seconds was almost suspended. In Victoria Street the storm burst with great violence, the electric fluid striking a chimney about 130 ft high, attached to the works under the street and facing the river, shivering the coping stones in all directions. The lightning also struck the chimney in two places lower down, tearing away consider-able portions of brickwork. Some of the falling stones fell upon the roof of the studio of Mr Warwick Brook, photo-graphic artist, breaking some of the plate glass in the win-dows, and destroying many of the bottles in which he kept his chemicals, and also did other serious damage. Happily no one was in the studio at the time. Many of the falling bricks and fragments of stones fell on the pavement in Victoria Street, and broke some of the flags. Two or three persons who were near the spot when the accident happened had narrow escapes for their lives, but with the exception of a man who it is said was knocked down and stunned, we have not been able to ascertain that any personal injury was caused. Many hundreds of people were attracted to the spot.'

Above: The dominating chimney stack from the river Irwell

Opposite top: Victoria Street in 1848, blighted by the Arches chimney

Opposite below: The base of the chimney and the buildings on Victoria Terrace on the corner of Cateaton Street and Victoria Street.
The photograph dated 1870 shows the buildings being demolished.

It was also reported that the chimney did not have a lightning conductor, unlike the Cathedral and other surrounding buildings. Correspondents to the Courier newspaper speculated on this act of negligence by the owners, Manchester Corporation, and what would have happened if a private company had shown similar irresponsibility. It was suggested that it should be made compulsory for all tall buildings and structures to have a lightning conductor. Further details emerged about the narrow escapes that day. Some had been sheltering in a doorway close to the chimney when falling masonry weighing an estimated hundredweight crashed down just a few feet away, smashing the pavement.

At Brook's photographic studio, a huge piece of masonry fell on the spot where, shortly before, people were sitting to have their portrait taken. In an adjoining hotel, the pan being washed by a servant was cut in two by a falling brick. The presence of the damaged chimney also highlighted the fact that this ugly piece of industrial architecture was obscuring the view of the Cathedral, one of the city's finest buildings.

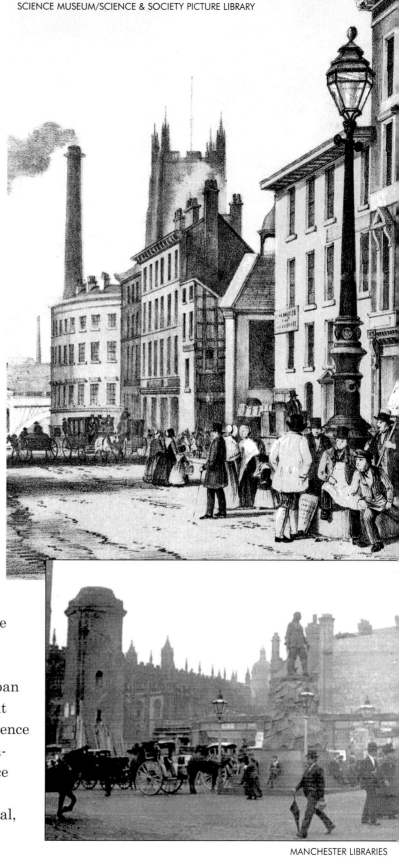

MANCHESTER LIBRARIES

Victoria Arches tenants

1840
Robert Armstrong - engineer

1841
Robert Armstrong - Civil Engineer & machine maker, office
Thomas Larmuth - machine maker
Arthur Burgess & Co - steam printers & 2 other occupants

1842
T Coatman & Son - manufacturer of Rowley's Patent Centrifugal pump, fire and steam engine

1843
Robert Armstrong - engineer, inventor of sedimentary collectors
John Coatman & Son - millwright/engineer (business closed 1844)
Arthur Burgess & Co - letterpress printers

1845
Robert Armstrong - civil engineer, Victoria Arches, office
Grenfell Pasco & Sons - copper merchants
(Thomas) Lister & (Jerry) Lees - ironmongers/iron merchants (wholesale and retail), stone grate manufacturers,
Sunlow & Berry - furnishing ironmongers, tin plate workers, braziers, locksmiths, bell hangers, gas fitters and fire-proof safe manufacturers
A Burgess & Co - letter-press printers (also at 28 Cross St)

1847
Grenfell Pasco & sons - copper & metal merchants
Williamson & Coldbeck - silk finishers & dyers
Sudlow & Berry - iron manufacturers
Arthur Burgess & co - engineers

1848
Robert Armstrong - civil engineer. House, New Bridge St,
Strangeways - business taken over by William Oxley, Bale Street,M/c
Williamson & Coldbeck - silk finishers
Laybourne & Forsyth - letter press printers
Lister & Lees, ironmongers, 3-5 Cateaton Street
Arthur Burgess & Co - letter press printers (by power)

1849
Thomas Larmuth - machine maker
(Berrys auction of tools etc 17 March 1849)
(Laybourne & Forsyth - letter press printers closed by April 1849)
Lister & Lees, ironmongers, 3-5 Cateaton Street
Arthur Burgess & Co - letter press printers (by power)

STEAM PRINTING OFFICES, VICTORIA ARCHES.—
S. A. *Burgess and Co.* are in immediate WANT of an APPRENTICE, with whom a premium will be required; also a Youth, who writes a good hand, for the office; and a respectable Girl, about 16 years of age.

Arthur Burgess

His printing company was first listed at the Arches in 1841. By 1847, he also had a bookbinding business at Back Pool Fold, 28 Cross Street. In an accident at his print shop at Victoria Arches in April 1843, an apprentice was severely injured when his apron caught in the cog wheels of the machinery. He was taken to the Infirmary where he later died.

In 1850, Burgess was on the committee of the Freehold Land Society for Manchester and the Northern Counties. That same year he went into partnership with William Frederick Peck, a printer and stationer at 29 Downing Street Ardwick. This arrangement lasted until March 1853 when their printing and engraving partnership was dissolved.

He was an active member of the Broughton Ratepayers' meeting, and wrote several letters to the Guardian regarding local issues. He was the elected member for the Kersal Ward in 1860. In 1841 Burgess and family were at Bloomsbury Terrace Lower Broughton, and by 1851 Arthur, his wife Mary, and son and six daughters lived at Bloomsbury Cottage, Broughton. By 1861 they had moved to 1 Exmouth Place, Lower Broughton Road, Broughton. He died in 1864 age 57.

Above: 1844 ad - possibly a replacement apprentice after the fatal accident

1850
Burgess & Peck - engravers & letterpress printers
Grenfell Pasco & Co - copper roller manufacturers,

1851
Williamson & Coldbeck - silk finishers & dyers
(Wm) Lees & Lister engineers
(Thomas Lister- retired from business March 1851) Arthur Burgess
& (Wm Fred) Jack - engineers
Greenfell Copper co - engineers

1857

VICTORIA ARCHES. -TO BE LET, No. 1 (117ft. by 20ft. 9in.) and No. 2 ARCH (101ft. 9in. by 21ft. 4in.) lately in the occupation of Benjamin Greening; also No. 3 (50ft. by 20ft. 8in) and No. 4 Arch (22ft. 6in. by 17ft. 6in.) with 15-horse power engine, boiler house, boiler, and office over passage, lately in the occupation of Samuel Hamer. No. 1 and 2 arch suitable for ale, porter, or wine stores.—Applications to be made to the City Treasurer, Town Hall, King-street.

1859
Cameron & co (agents for Worthington & Robinson brewers)

1860 -1861
Joseph Renshaw - engineer, machinist
& six other tenants

1863
Grenfell Pasco & Sons - copper merchants, Hunts Bank & 33 George Street (partnership dissolved 1871)

1873
GW Simpole - cotton flock dealer
Robert Oats - coppersmith

1874

LARGE Well-lighted STORES, Victoria Arches, under Victoria-street.— J. E. HARLEY, Town Hall, King-street

1877- 1879
Luke Daniel - joiner
Frederick Johnson - joiner & builder
(James)Taylor (Joseph) Sherwood & Co - pickle manufacturers,

1881
William Archer - gas apparatus manufacturer for the Gas Meter Co Ltd,

James Sinclair - furnace engineer & smoke preventor manufacturers (of chemical fire engines, rotary fire escapes, smoke respirators, and general fire apparatus. Cathedral Steps, Victoria Street
Frederick Johnson - joiner & builder & 5 other tenants

1882
William Archer
James Sinclair - chemical engine maker
Charles Simpole - cabinet maker

1883
Luke Daniel - undertaker
William Archer - engineer
Thomas Bradford & Co - churn makers, sewing machine maker & dealer, iron founder, removed from Cathedral Steps

1885 -1886
William Archer

1887-89
Charles Simpole - furniture dealer, Cathedral Yard, Victoria Arches

1890 - 1897
Executors of Charles Simpole

1901
Mayor & Alderman - workshop
Thomas Cook & Son - shop

1907-20
Electricity Dept - workshop (re-assessed and divided)
Thomas Cook & Son - shop

1921-22
Electricity Dept - workshop
Thomas Cook & Son (Thos Frank Henry, Ernest Edward) - office & underground store

1931-32
No reference to Electricity Dept - workshop in rates book
Thomas Cook & Son - office & underground store

1936-1957
Electricity Dept - transformer station

● *The listings based on available directories and rates books.*

161

The Victoria and Cathedral
landing stages by the Arches

IRWELL EXCURSIONS

Ferry services began in 1895 from landing stages at the
Arches. Boats from the Irwell Steam Ferry Company and
the Ship Canal Passenger Steamer Company began trips
up the Irwell from around the 27 May. The two
companies had already begun trips the previous year
along the Ship Canal. The Irwell Steam Ferry Company
ran a service from the Albert Bridge stage with new boats
'Nellie' and 'Amy' which began in May. By August, the
other company had a fleet of ten boats including 'Pioneer'
and 'Nelly' plying from Albert Bridge to the docks, Barton
and Irlam. The fare to the docks was 3p. They also had
larger boats - the former cross-Channel steamer 'Dynamic',
'Australia', 'Manx Fairy', 'St Mawes Castle' and Scottish
steamer 'John Stirling', departing from Trafford Wharf up
the Ship Canal to Lymm, and special bank holiday sailings
to Liverpool and New Brighton .

Encouraged by the growing number of visitors to
the docks, it was announced in February 1895 that
passengers would soon be able to embark from the
new landing stage from the more central position of
the Arches close to the Exchange and Victoria railway
stations. The Irwell Steam Ferry owners had ordered
new boats for the shallower waters further up river.

The landing stages known as the 'Victoria' and
'Cathedral' were floating platforms which adjusted to the
level of the river, with separate steps and booking offices
for the rival companies. For the service to begin, the river
had to be dredged to create an adequate depth of water.
Crowds had watched as several feet of cinders tipped into
the river over the years were removed from the river bed.

Sailings from the Victoria Landing Stage were
at half-hour intervals between 10.30am and 5.30pm
to Manchester Docks, calling at Albert Bridge for more
passengers. There was also a cruise along the newly-
opened Manchester Ship Canal through Irlam, Lymm,
Runcorn and Frodsham to Eastham. Fares on the Ship
Canal Passenger Steamer Company boats were 3p single
and 5p return.

Boats to Australia

In February 1896, the Ship Canal
Passenger Steamer Company put its boats
up for sale. 'Water Lily', 'Manx Fairy' and
'St Mawes Castle' were sold to The
Western Australian Steam Packet and
Transport Company and set off on the
arduous journey to Perth. As they did not
have enough capacity for coal, they were rigged with
sails. 'St Mawes Castle' did not complete the voyage.
She left Liverpool for Capetown on 14 March, and sailed
from Table Bay on 11 July, but was never seen again.

Chilling entry in the the Shipping
Register - the missing 'St Mawes
Castle' was no longer insurable

Another four went to Scottish buyers John James Neil and Arthur Harlow, and the final four to the Irwell Steam Ferry Company, owned by Edward Rowland, and underwent a complete refit. The Company also acquired the other landing stage at Victoria. The public were notified that the recent practice of flexible starting times, such as waiting until sufficient numbers were on board, would stop and boats would set off at the advertised time. The Company had also bought the offices and landing stage at Albert Bridge, and its vessels would stop at Regent Road, Pomona Docks, Trafford Wharf and Mode Wheel. From 2-16 March 1896, the new timetable was: every hour from 11am to 5pm, and then from 16-31 March every half hour from 10.30am to 5.30pm. The time-table altered slightly through the summer months. They also offered a daily trip to Barton at 3.30pm.

Extra steamers were advertised the following summer, with excursions to the Trafford Park fête and the chance to see an old convict ship berthed at Pomona Dock on which the conditions of the inmates one hundred years previously were re-created. Steamers were leaving the Victoria stage every twenty minutes, and there was an additional 11am trip to Barton. Special attractions in 1899 were 'Barnum's Great Show' at Trafford Park, and the steamer 'Ernest Bazin' on rollers at the docks.

'Open sewer'

The sailings in 1900 which included trips to the Botanical Gardens at Old Trafford were to be the last. Two major factors are said to have caused the end of the service: the lack of punctuality of the boats and the unpleasant quality of the water stirred up by the paddles and propellers of the steamers on this notoriously polluted river, described at the time as 'little more than an open sewer'. In a report to the Manchester and Salford Sanitary Association in 1891, Consulting Chemist

Boats damaged

In February 1899 two of the Irwell Steam Ferry Company's boats 'Annie' and 'Maud' moored at the landing stage at Albert Bridge were damaged when a barge broke loose from its moorings at Blackfriars Bridge during bad weather. The barge, which had not been securely tied, was taken by the swollen river and hit the two steamers, which were dashed against Albert Bridge. The owner of the barge paid £77 in compensation for the damage.

William Thompson wrote: '... I observed along the river that gas was being liberated from the putrefying mud at the bottom coming constantly to the surface'. An engineer's report to the Association stated '.. at Hunt's Bank where the Irk joins, there is another large bank of foul mud.'

The 'grim' river trips were remembered by a newspaper writer in 1906: *'The cruise along the inky river between the black and frowning warehouse walls, steep to the water, which towards the end of the passage gave place only to a wider prospect of desolation - grimy, blighted, industrial wilderness, - was a sensation worth experiencing. Even the showers of smut over the passengers was in keeping with the Stygian scene, but neither that nor anything else was of a nature to attract the season ticket holder.'*

The Albert Bridge landing stage was put up for sale in September 1900. By 1901, six pleasure steamers were moored by the Arches. At around two o'clock on the afternoon of the 12 November they were buffeted by a severe storm and one of the vessels, 'Maud' on the outside berth, partially sank as large pieces of timber, possibly supports from a nearby bridge, made a hole in the side of the boat. Large crowds gathered to watch the spectacle as the engine room was swamped with water, but fortunately additional ropes were attached which prevented the boat from sinking. Spectators also saw uprooted trees, barrels, and cattle carried down the swollen river, which had risen nearly six feet. The unused landing stages were removed in November 1906, and many were drawn to watch the rats, which had inhabited the landing stage, making for the river. Workmen threw stones at them as they tried to recongregate on a narrow sandbank on the opposite side of the river.

Captain honoured

Joseph Bosley, captain of the boat 'Annie' was awarded 'the honourable testimonial' of the Royal Humane Society, following his rescue of a youth who had fallen into the river from the bridge by the Palatine Buildings in July 1900. It emerged at the award ceremony that the captain had saved the lives of fifteen others - reminiscent of the exploits of Mark Addy who had rescued over fifty people from the Irwell. 'Annie' is seen here in service later at Maldon, Essex.

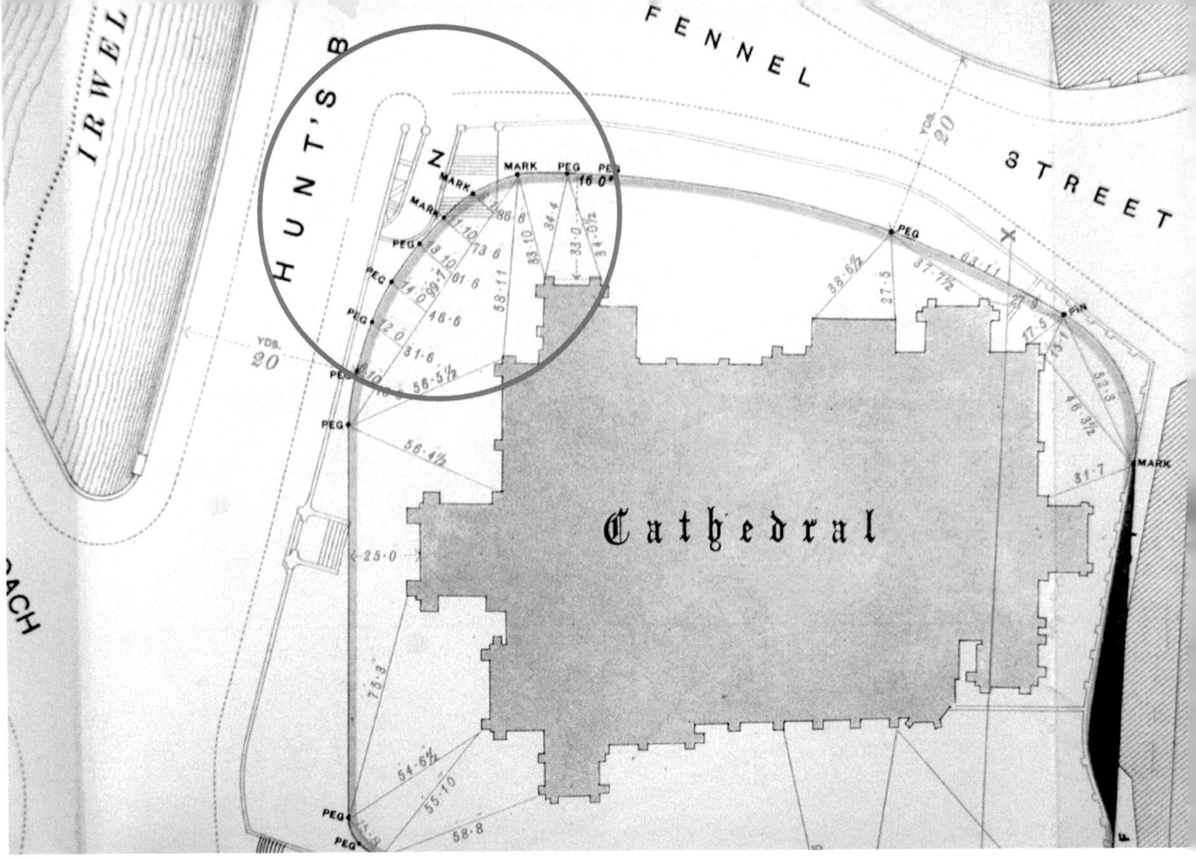

In 1894 the Cathedral wall was altered to improve the surrounding roads and walkways. The agreement between the Corporation and Cathedral authorities stipulated that the entrance (circled) into the Arches had to remain as it was.

The 1836 dramatic collapse of the river wall by the Arches was not to be the last, because in December 1939 a thirty-yard length of the road and river wall fell into the Irwell. The section of the wall affected was opposite Palatine buildings and occurred at 8am. Two teenagers were standing at a bus stop as the pavement suddenly gave way beneath them and the roadway subsided. The girls, surrounded by tumbling masonry, were taken around 30ft down to the river level but, amazingly, were unscathed because they fell onto the debris rather than into the river. A passing van-boy from Victoria Station parcel department hauled the first girl to safety with a rope, and the second who was partially disabled, was helped back by the Fire Service with a ladder.

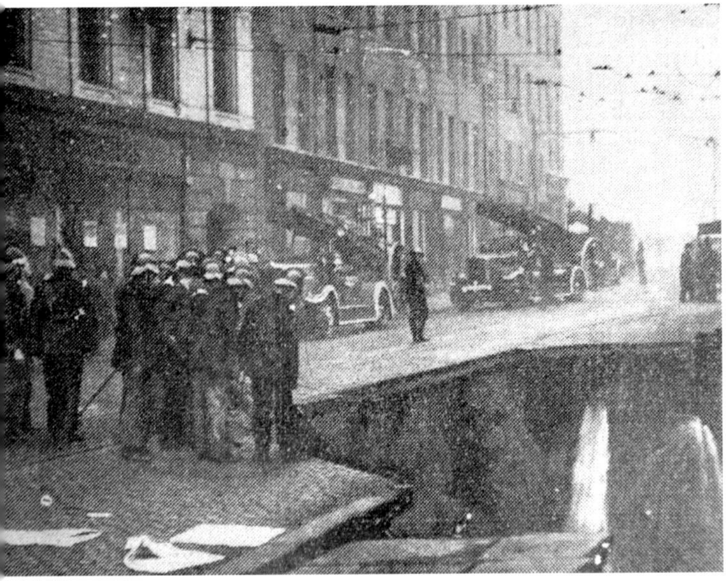

The latter girl described the experience as 'like falling through a trap-door' and that the noise was 'terrifying'. Both girls were treated for shock and bruising and were discharged from hospital the same day. The subsidence broke two water mains and an eighteen-inch gas main as well as demolishing a telephone kiosk, a tramway standard, paving stones and granite setts. A motor cyclist was thrown off his bike by the collapse but only suffered slight bruising. It was thought that the flooded basements of the furniture store in Palatine Buildings were the cause of the subsidence. The consequences of the incident could have been much worse because only a few moments earlier a crowded bus had passed over the site of the collapse.

Hero - Wilfred Schofield who helped to rescue the two casualties.

It seems the strength of the wall had never been totally trusted by successive city engineers. When the King and Queen visited Manchester in 1905 and on previous occasions, a temporary wooden fence was erected in front of the iron railings.

ELECTRICITY DEPARTMENT

About 1901, the Arches were newly occupied by the Corporation as a workshop for the Electricity Department where tests and investigations were made on electrical equipment. They also used it as a battery-testing station and by March 1902 it had cost £6,634 to set up. Between 1907 and 1909 the battery station had a yearly expenditure of £1237 12s 1p.

Thomas Cook and Son had a shop in the premises built onto the Arches by Victoria Bridge. Cook's had expanded by 1921 and were also renting space at the southern end of the Arches for offices and storage.

After the last World War, the department was reorganised into the North Western Electricity Board and both the Electricity Board and Thomas Cook are listed in the rates records at the Arches until 1957. In the later years, access to the testing station was via the steps over the river wall. The northern cartway entrance had been closed off by 1905.

War time preparations - a new entrance to the shelter on Victoria Street

WAR TIME

The Arches were in good structural condition when they came under consideration as an air-raid shelter during the last world war. City Engineer's report concentrated on installing new entrances, flooring, seating and lighting.

It was found that arches 5-7 were only accessible from the toilets, and for arches A to F and 1-3 the sole entrance was through a manhole in the main passage through the arches. A flight of steps by the Cromwell statue to arches A-F and 1-3 was suggested, along with

168

additional access to other arches by steps in front
of the Cathedral. An internal flight of steps from the
passage to arch 3 would connect two sets of arches.

The Arches shelter was intended for those within ten
minutes' walk - an area bounded by Miller Street, High
Street, and Bridge Street. Based on national guidelines,
the shelter could hold up to 1030 people for 6 hours
in unventilated conditions, or as many as 5600 in
an emergency if ventilated.

War time sign at one of
the entrances to the shelter

The entrances would be from Victoria
Bridge by a wooden stairway; Victoria
Street junction with Fennel Street by
a flight of steps formed under the pavement, and from the Cathedral approach
by means of a wooden stairway from the
existing conveniences. The entrances
would be air-locked and the openings in
the arches overlooking the River Irwell
would be filled in and made gas-proof.
A second report on 27 January 1939
concluded the Arches could be converted
into a blast and splinter-proof shelter
for 3,300 people. A ventilation system
with air filters would remove gas, using fans driven by
an electric motor with a diesel engine as a standby. All
the work would cost £8,000 and would take three months
to complete. The outline of the scheme had been given
approval by the Home Office on the 25 October 1938.
A revised, more detailed estimate of the 10 July 1939
put the cost of converting the Arches at £10,150.

At the time of the inspection the names of some of the
businesses which had used the Arches could still be seen
painted on the walls. On the 7 January 1939 a scheme
for a pedestrian subway under Victoria Street between

169

Above: War time building work at the Arches

Opposite: Shelter notice indicating anti-social behaviour is not a new thing

Below: Outline plan of the Arches

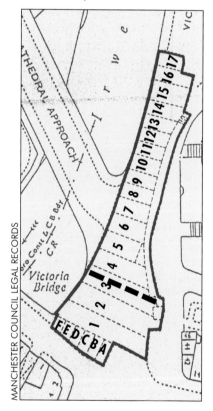

Cathedral Yard and Exchange Station was submitted by the traffic congestion committee. The estimated cost was £4000 and in March 1939 it was forwarded to the Air Raid Precautions Committee for consideration with the scheme for the air-raid shelters. Home Office approval was received by 20 June 1939, and instructions for the work to commence were given on 27 August 1939. The work was carried out by Wellerman Brothers Ltd of Sheffield for £11,093 17s 4d.

1950s INSPECTION

After the war, the Arches were inspected in May 1951 by Mr TB Sprowson of the Ministry of Works for potential use as Air-Raid Shelters by the Regional Civil Defence.

They could accommodate 562 on bunks, along with 1057 seated - a total of 1619 persons. A water, electricity and sewer system was installed in Arch 4 but disconnected from the other arches. The gas supply was close to the entrance. All the arches except 9 and 10 (electricity sub-station) were to be used for accommodation. The estimated cost to adapt the Arches was £3,622.

The report also stated that Arch 5 had been used for a time after the war as a ladies' public toilet. The proposed subway through to Arch 4 and the access stairways at each end were never built.

The overhead protection varied from 3ft 9in to 7ft 6in over the crowns of the arches. A 500lb MC bomb could perforate and 'blow through' if it made a direct hit over the crown of the arch. Nevertheless, the Arches were deemed 'safe' and suitable for shelter accommodation.

NCHESTER CITY POLICE.

AIR RAID PRECAUTIONS.

OTICE

AIR RAID SHELTERS have been
tructed throughout the City or the protection
tizens and other persons without protection
g AIR ATTACK, and members of the public
sked to co operate with the Local Authority
sisting the Police and Wardens in ensuring
proper use and mainte ance.

The rules for **GOOD CONDUCT** of
nc lters, mindful of the fact that
ns n sexes, young and old, may be
ection, demand

SMOK.

INSOBRIETY

GAMBLING

OBSCENE LANGUAGE

ROWD

UNSE NDUCT

gs will be taken ag rsons found
ly ishig shel or th rules. It should
cessary to reso t to ana estly desired that
bers of the pu lic w ed o MUNITY, interest
es i the colle t e effo to sure that G UCT is

ice, ice,
tr
TER.
o

MAXWELL,
Chief Constable.

Manchester. 1 W.S.

Remains of the Arches' war-time use as an air raid shelter

Left top: Warden's post

Above left and below: Medical posts

Above: The main passage from Victoria Street to the Arches shelter. It was later used by the public as a through way. This was originally the cartway where the various businesses brought their goods and raw materials in and out.

Opposite: Remnants of war-time and possible previous use by the electricity department

Right: The Public conveniences in the Arches continued to be used after the last war. Toilets had been discussed for this site in 1899.

Manchester and Salford Junction Canal tunnel

Wandering around the tunnel today, it is easy to forget that for a few years it was crammed with people sheltering from enemy bombing. This section describes what it was like to be down here in those troubled times; also, the people who built and managed the tunnel, how the tunnel was built, and the incidents in the tunnel and on the canal.

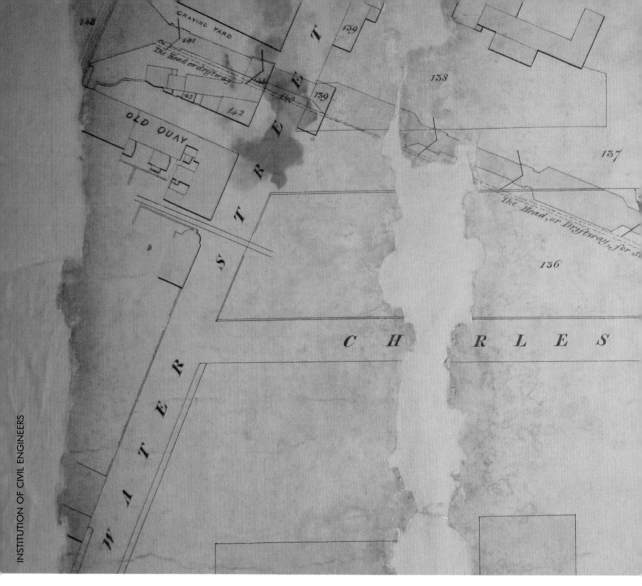

The map shows a detailed plan with labels including:

- 148
- GRAVING YARD
- 159
- The Head or Driftway
- 142
- 140
- 159
- 158
- OLD QUAY
- 137
- The Head, or Driftway, for s...
- 136
- WATER STREET
- CHARLES

The first section of the Manchester and Salford Junction Canal where it links with the River Irwell, drawn up in 1835.

An independent company largely composed of shareholders from the Mersey and Irwell Navigation Company promoted the cutting of the canal across the centre of Manchester to link the Mersey and Irwell with the Rochdale Canal. It was envisaged as a profitable undertaking which would also help reduce traffic congestion in the city. The original plans to estimate costs were drawn up by John Nightingale in 1805. He was also the resident engineer on the Manchester, Bolton and Bury Narrow Canal which opened in 1808. It was to be a further thirty years before the Manchester and Salford Junction Canal was built, but in 1824 land was purchased by the Mersey

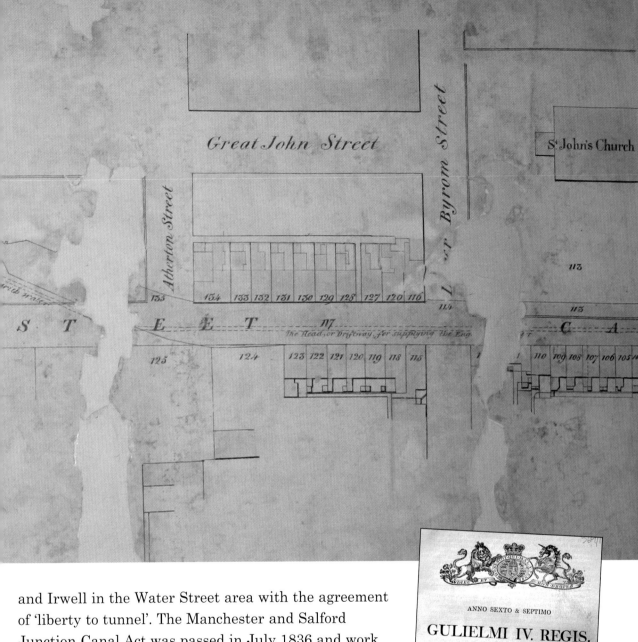

Great John Street

St John's Church

and Irwell in the Water Street area with the agreement of 'liberty to tunnel'. The Manchester and Salford Junction Canal Act was passed in July 1836 and work began a year later.

The Act reveals interesting details of the building and running of the canal. For example, gunpowder could not be used in the tunnel construction; the penalty for usage was £50. The tunnel was not to pass beneath St John's churchyard. The 1835 drawing showed that at least in the early stages of planning, the tunnel did infringe the church grounds. The Act also stipulated that the water

ANNO SEXTO & SEPTIMO

GULIELMI IV. REGIS.

Cap. cxv.

An Act for making and maintaining a navigable Canal to connect the *Rochdale* Canal and the River *Irwell* in the Township of *Manchester* in the County of *Lancaster.*　　[4th July 1836.]

WHEREAS the Towns of *Bolton* and *Bury* in the County Palatine of *Lancaster*, and their respective Neighbourhoods, are very populous, and contain therein extensive Mills for the Spinning of Cotton and Flax, and other manufacturing and commercial Establishments, and the Population and Manufactures of the said Towns and Neighbourhoods respectively have of late Years very considerably increased : And whereas Goods and Merchandize to a considerable Extent are now carried and conveyed by Carts and Waggons along the Streets in *Manchester*, from the *Manchester, Bolton,* and *Bury* Canal and the River *Irwell* to the *Rochdale* Canal, and thereby the Passage along such Streets is frequently impeded : And whereas the making and maintaining a navigable Canal from the *Rochdale* Canal in the Township of *Manchester* in the Parish of *Manchester* in the said County of *Lancaster* to and communicating with the River *Irwell* at the Graving Yard of the Company of Proprietors of the *Mersey* and *Irwell* Navigation would be of great Public Utility : And whereas the several Persons herein-after named are desirous of being united into a Company for making the said navigable Canal and Branch, but the same cannot be accomplished without
[*Local.*]　　　　　　　37 N　　　　　　　the

181

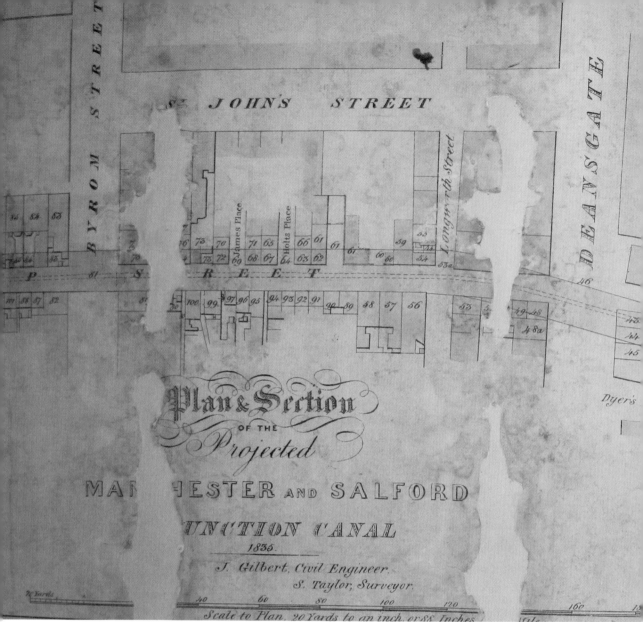

BYROM STREET

ST. JOHN'S STREET

DEANSGATE

Longworth Street

James Place

Holts Place

Dyer's

Plan & Section
OF THE
Projected
MANCHESTER AND SALFORD
JUNCTION CANAL
1835.
J. Gilbert, Civil Engineer.
S. Taylor, Surveyor.

70 Yards   40   60   80   100   120   160

Scale to Plan. 20 Yards to an inch, or 88 Inches

level in the canal had to be at least six inches above the level of the Rochdale Canal at all times, and that no water was to be taken from the Rochdale Canal. This was to safeguard the interests of the Rochdale Canal Company and caused much expense to maintain levels in the MSJC, with the need for pumping engines and a reservoir. Preparations were being finalised in 1835 with a plan surveyed by S Taylor and drawn up by John Gilbert, a civil engineer who had been involved in the Bridgewater Canal scheme. Later, Thomas Fletcher

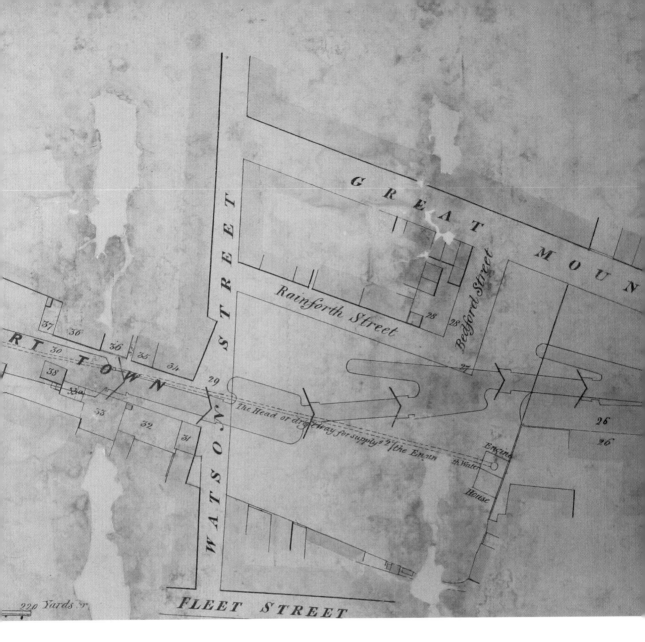

became the engineer and agent on the Junction Canal project. The main contractor, William Mackenzie (1794-1851), was one of the first international railway contractors, with not only projects such as the Lime Street Tunnel on the Liverpool Manchester Railway, but also railways in mainland Europe.

The 1835 plan was to be modified because it showed a proposed branch canal off the Rochdale Canal ending at New Worcester Street, near Cambridge Street, after pass-

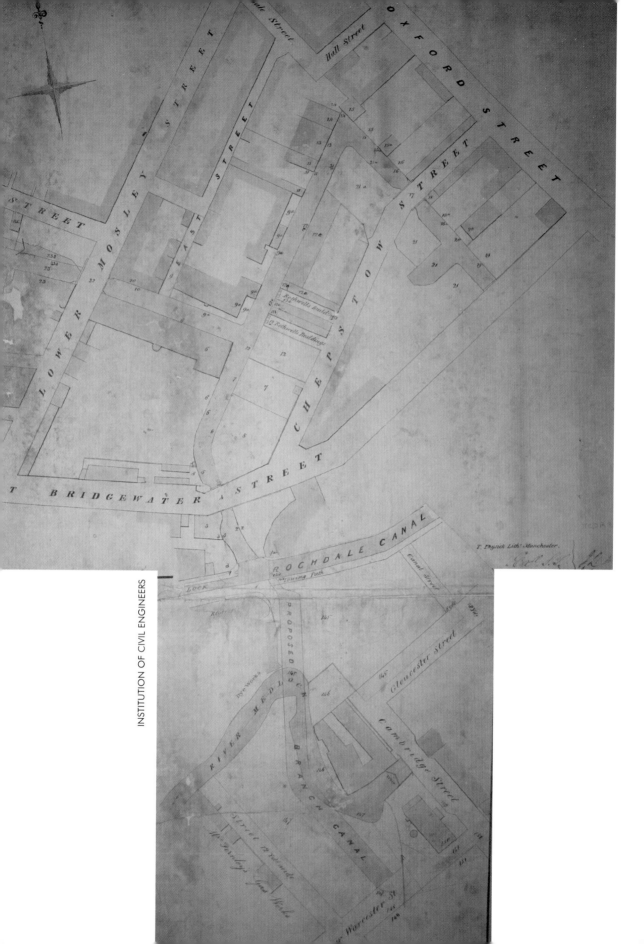

ing over the River Medlock. Also, the canal was to have double locks but this plan shows singles where it comes in off the River Irwell and at Watson Street. In the final scheme the engine house and water tunnel were on the north bank of the canal. These were a part of many alterations to the original plans which were scrutinised by the city authorities. In general the plans were approved, although some modifications were required to the brickwork of the driftway - the tunnels which supplied water to the pumping engines, and provision had to be made for the diversion of gas pipes and sewers.

Work commenced with the breaking of ground at both ends of the 1100 yard long canal in July 1837. The digging of the tunnel was done from both ends, and a through passage was completed towards the end of April 1838. 26,000 yards of excavation were required.

At the lower end, the canal commenced in the graving yard of the Old Quay Company. In the first lock at Water Street, the water level was raised six feet. The next were double locks, which were unusual because vessels could be worked both ways without the loss of water. The canal then entered the 511 yard-long tunnel. This was 20 ft wide, and the depth of the water was 8ft 6in. The height from the surface of the water to the centre of the arch was 11ft 6in. The towing path, which was excavated out of the solid rock, was 3ft 6in wide. When the canal came into the open, it passed through another set of double locks by the Dacca Mills before ascending to a connection with a branch of the Rochdale Canal. It then passed under Great Bridgewater Street before joining the main Rochdale Canal at Tib Lock.

The safety aspects were emphasised by the builders, with fencing by the canal to prevent accidents. Also, because so much of the canal's route was underground, it was thought to be inaccessible to the public and therefore not a hazard. However, a series of accidents later suggested that it was not as safe as at first thought.

The Rope and Anchor public house on Water Street was demolished around January 1838 to make way for tunnel construction, and the publican's licence was transferred to premises near the railway station. The site of the entrance to the canal had been used by the Mersey and Irwell Company to build and repair barges. The business moved to the Water Street end of the canal and continued until the 1930s.

The work progressed well with little public inconvenience and pleasant surprise was expressed in the Guardian newspaper in February 1838 that Mr Mackenzie expected the tunnel to be completed in a few weeks, and that the canal would be ready by the end of September. Mr Mackenzie's optimism was reasonably accurate and the canal was officially opened on 28 October 1839.

OPENING

A notice and map advertising the opening of the route and the tonnage rates charged, also listed the key selling points of the route. There were double locks which helped to speed up traffic, gas lamps every 20 yards, and a towing path, and men available for hauling vessels for the maximum charge of 6 pence or a farthing a ton.

RATES OF TONNAGE, &c.

JUNCTION CANAL.

| On all Articles, Matters, and Things, carried or conveyed upon the whole length of this Canal | 6d. ℔ Ton. |

On all Articles, Matters, and Things, carried or conveyed from either end, to the entrance of the Tunnel nearest Water-street .... 3d. ℔ Ton.

N.B. No Vessel to pay for a less weight than four tons, unless the same shall be returning unloaded after having passed through the Canal loaded.

MERSEY AND IRWELL NAVIGATION.

On all Articles, Matters, and Things, carried or conveyed from the Junction Canal into the Bolton and Bury Canal .... 1½d. ℔ Ton.

On all Articles, Matters, and Things, carried or conveyed from the Bolton and Bury Canal into the Junction Canal .... Free.

N.B. It is arranged that all Articles, Matters, and Things coming through the Junction Canal, and using *this* Navigation to Liverpool, Runcorn, Warrington, or elsewhere, shall be charged exactly the same rate of tonnage as though they had been conveyed upon the Bridgewater Canal.

OPENING OF THE MANCHESTER and SALFORD JUNCTION CANAL.—The Public are respectfully informed, that the MANCHESTER and SALFORD JUNCTION CANAL, connecting the river Irwell, near the Old Quay, with the Rochdale Canal, near the Albion Mills; and, by means of existing navigations, the western coast, at Liverpool, with the eastern coast, at Hull, and the several intermediate districts, will be OPEN to the PUBLIC, on and after MONDAY the 28th instant.—By order of the Committee,
WILLM. SLATER,
18th Oct. 1839.
Law-clerk.

William Mackenzie, the contractor, kept a diary of his busy working life. The following entries indicate further work had been required on the tunnel after it opened for traffic:

Monday 13 January 1840 (fine day)
'...arrived in Manchester at 9.15am, called at Tunnel, saw Street getting on with the underpinning at the Tunnel ...'

Thursday 23 January 1840 (rain and wind)
'Went to Manchester over the Junction Canal Works, underpinning half done ...'

Wed 12 Feb 1840 (fine)
'Went to the Manchester Junction Canal works, inspected tunnel where opened from surface at Camp Street, found all good ...'

Tuesday 4 August 1840 (very fine)
'I went to Manchester, attended Junction Canal meeting. Wanted account settling, put off three weeks longer.'

Thursday 15 October 1840
'Went to Manchester, met Shorland*, commenced measuring Junction Canal Works'

Monday 3 May 1841
'Betts and I went to Manchester, arrived at 10.30am, met Fletcher, afterwards Shorland and son, went over Canal accounts, finished about 5pm, dined at Westall's and left by 7pm train'

Monday 17 May 1841
'Met Shorland, went over Canal bills ...'

*George Shorland was the city authority surveyor for the Police Commissioners

INSTITUTION OF CIVIL ENGINEERS

William Mackenzie

Mackenzie worked with another contractor, William Betts, on the tunnel and shared the profits on the £47,000 contract.

DROWNINGS

Despite the efforts to promote the canal as safe, it was not too long before a nine year old boy drowned in its waters during May 1840. He and two friends were playing in Water Street with two planks floating on the canal when he overbalanced and fell in. His friends could not rescue him and ran off in panic. The boy's father was notified and his son's body was found after draining the water from the section of the canal. The boy, Henry Gill, was the son of a shoemaker who lived in a cellar beneath 10 Gartside Street.

Canal reopening advertisement 27 May 1840

The canal was closed for several months while the top lock was rebuilt to the correct specification. It reopened on Monday 29 May 1840. Further works were carried out after an Act of 1841 allowed construction of a branch from the canal bounded by Water Street, Quay Street and Atherton Street to link with a potato market.

The traffic expected by the canal's promoters did not materialise. They had been hampered by potential business being diverted through the newly opened Hulme Locks from the Bridgewater Canal to the Rochdale at more favourable rates just before the MSJC opened. Then there were problems with pumping engines and a collapsed lock wall, which also contributed to the already extensive costs in constructing the canal and tunnel. We have an insight into the company's finances in a rates appeal in 1841. It was stated by the Manchester and Salford Canal Company that the annual income from the canal was £1,135 16s 3d, whereas the annual expenditure amounted to £1,775 17s 3d.

The failing canal was offered to the Mersey and Irwell Company in 1841 for £30,750 along with debts of over £20,000. When this was declined, it was re-offered and accepted on the basis of only taking over the works. The Mersey and Irwell were taken over in 1844 by the Bridgewater Company, who had no need of the MSJC because of their own connection with the Rochdale Canal at Hulme Locks. However, the canal remained open for limited traffic.

Another tragedy occurred in October 1848 when Robert Harrison drowned in the canal while out playing with friends. In attempting to raise the lock gates to let a vessel through, he slipped and fell in the water. Every attempt was made to rescue him but with no success, and his body was recovered and taken to the Old Quay tavern, Water Street, where an inquest was later held and a verdict of accidental death returned.

The Potato Wharf at Brunswick Basin

POTATO ACCIDENT

In July 1850, a boat heavily laden with potatoes on its way to the potato wharf near Quay Street, overturned in the canal as it entered the locks. All thirteen on board survived the incident, which had been caused by the accidental raising of the lock gates which brought a rush of water. It happened at 11.20pm on a Friday. The water was drained off, and as many potatoes as possible were recovered by the crew.

A boatman named Samuel Bennett drowned in the canal after getting drunk. On a Wednesday in September 1850, in an intoxicated state, he had gone through the tunnel and then at Alport Town went to the Black Horse pub and fell asleep. Later he returned to look for his boat in the tunnel but not was seen again. The following Sunday afternoon, his body was discovered between two boats (one of which was his) coming out of the tunnel.

The 26 Rules of Navigation notice which was posted along the canal in 1874 gives an idea of how the route was supposed to operate. It stated in bold type that no vessel could be left without a person on board. Vessels had to have a light fore and aft, whatever time of day or night, when passing through the tunnel. Passenger packets had priority. Every steam vessel had to have a loud whistle which had to be sounded when approaching or overtaking another vessel, or when coming to a turning. Offences would be punished by up to six months jail with possible hard labour, or by a fine of up to £100.

CLOSURE

In 1875 the Cheshire Lines Committee Act authorized the sale, closure and filling-in of the canal between Watson Street and Lower Mosley Street. The previous year, the Cheshire Lines Committee and the railway companies had formed the Bridgewater Canal Company to take over the running of the canal and to acquire land between Deansgate and Lower Mosley Street. So that section of the canal to the Rochdale Canal was filled in, covering over the top locks and a reservoir. The remains of the canal were bought by the Manchester Ship Canal Company under the Ship Canal Act of 1885.

The Great Northern Warehouse was built over the canal in 1899 and two hoist wells built down to the canal provided a link between the railway and the docks. On the adjoining site, Central Station was built, and later two wagon hoists down to the tunnel from the station's goods yard also helped boost traffic.

By 1922 the route had again become disused, but the tunnel end of the canal continued to be used for barge repairs and engineering work for the Manchester Ship Canal Company until the 1930s. The Royal barge in which Queen Victoria travelled when she came to open

RULES

Made by Her Majesty the Queen, at a Court at Windsor, the 18th day of May, 1870, by virtue of the Powers vested in Her Majesty by the "Merchant Shipping Amendment Act, 1862," by and with the advice of Her Privy Council, concerning the Lights and Signals to be carried, and concerning the Steps to be taken by Vessels navigating the Inland Navigations called "THE DUKE OF BRIDGEWATER'S CANAL," "THE MANCHESTER AND SALFORD JUNCTION CANAL," "THE RUNCORN AND WESTON CANAL," and "THE MERSEY AND IRWELL NAVIGATION," or any of them.

1. In Her Majesty's said Order in Council, the term "vessel" includes ships, boats, barges, craft, packets, and vessels of every kind navigating or being upon or in any part of the Duke of Bridgewater's Canal, the Manchester and Salford Junction Canal, and the Runcorn and Weston Canal, or any of them, or on or in any cut, canal, or other works belonging to the said navigations or any of them.

2. No vessel shall be navigated on any of the said navigations referred to in the foregoing Order, without a rudder at the stern, unless duly authorised by some agent of the owners of, or body of persons interested in, the respective navigations on which the same shall be navigated.

3. No vessel shall be navigated without one person, at the least, on board, competent to steer and manage her, and acquainted with the ordinary rules of navigating on canals.

4. **No vessel shall lie or be left without a person on board capable of taking care thereof.**

5. No vessel shall be navigated through a tunnel, either by day or by night, without carrying a light visible fore and aft.

6. Nothing shall be allowed to project beyond the sides of any vessel.

7. No vessel shall be placed or lie so as to obstruct the passage of any other vessel into or out of any lock, dock, bridgeway, stop-place, aqueduct, or tunnel, or enter any such lock, dock, bridgeway, stop-place, aqueduct, or tunnel, out of its turn.

8. **No vessel shall remain or be placed so as to obstruct the passage upon and along any part of the said canals respectively.**

9. No vessel shall be moored in any dock entrance, bridgeway, stop-place, aqueduct, or tunnel.

10. No attempt shall be made to moor a vessel in any basin, dock, or cut, or near any wharf, warehouse, or crane, contrary to the orders of an agent of the owners of, or body interested in, the said navigations respectively.

11. Every vessel which would, if not stopped, meet another vessel on a part of any of the said navigations where two vessels cannot pass each other, shall stop at the passage place, until the other vessel shall have passed clear of her.

12. No vessel shall be or remain at the entrance to any dock or basin, or in any bridgeway, stop-place, aqueduct, or tunnel, or at any crane or wharf, longer than is necessary for passing through or using the same.

13. No attempt shall be made so to load, unload, moor, or berth any vessel in any lock, dock, basin, bridgeway, stop-place, tunnel, or aqueduct, or so near thereto as to obstruct the passage thereof.

14. The line of every vessel going down the navigation shall be lowered and give way to every passing vessel going up the navigation, unless the vessel going down the navigation is a passenger packet, in which case the vessel going up the navigation and not being a passenger packet shall give way to the passenger packet.

15. The line of every vessel not being a passenger packet, and whether light or loaded, shall be lowered and give way to a passenger packet.

16. Every vessel not being a passenger packet shall, whenever a passenger packet is within one hundred yards from any lock, bridge, aqueduct, or tunnel give way to such passenger packet, and let it pass first through such lock, bridge, aqueduct, or tunnel.

17. There shall be a driver in attendance upon every horse hauling any vessel, or being upon any hauling-road or towing-path.

18. Every steam vessel shall be furnished with a loud and shrill steam whistle, and such steam whistle shall be placed before the funnel, not less than three feet above the deck or gunwale of such vessel, and shall be so fitted that it shall be blown by the steam from the boiler of the vessel.

19. The steam whistle of every vessel under steam shall be sounded as follows, viz., when such vessel is about to round, and is rounding any turnings in the navigation, as well as when such vessel is meeting, approaching, or overtaking any vessel.

20. Every vessel under steam, when passing a vessel not under steam, shall pass the vessel not under steam on the off-side thereof.

21. Every vessel not under steam shall take the towing-path side when meeting or passing, or approaching to, or being overtaken by, a vessel under steam.

22. Every vessel under steam meeting another vessel under steam shall, if going down the navigation, take the off-side, and shall, if coming up the navigation, take the towing-path side.

23. Every vessel under steam overtaking another vessel under steam shall take the off-side.

24. Every vessel under steam, when being overtaken by another vessel under steam, shall take the towing-path side.

25. Every vessel under steam shall check her speed when meeting, overtaking, or approaching any vessel, and shall stop and reverse if necessary.

26. No person shall, without being duly authorised by some agent of the owners of, or body interested in, the said several navigations respectively, cut any mooring line, or unmoor or cut adrift any vessel.

N. B.—The said Merchant Shipping Act, 1862, enacts that all Owners and Masters and other persons having command or charge of any Vessel are to take notice of the foregoing rules, and will for every infringement thereof be guilty of a **MISDEMEANOUR**, and liable to be punished (on summary conviction) by **IMPRISONMENT** for any period not exceeding **SIX CALENDAR MONTHS** with or without hard labour, or by a **PENALTY** not exceeding £100.

E. LEADER WILLIAMS, Jun.,
GENERAL MANAGER.

Bridgewater Navigation Offices,
Manchester, June 1st, 1874.

the first lock on the Manchester Ship Canal used to be tied up at the Grape Street end of the canal tunnel. This was Lord Ellesmere's state barge which was occasionally used to entertain guests, with trotting horses ridden by jockey-boys pulling the boat.

A Guardian article described the canal tunnel in July 1931 as abandoned and frequented occasionally by young people. 'Today the narrow towpath is officially boarded up, but there is a gap in the woodwork through which the agile may creep. Those who work near the entrance hint darkly of parties of youths who steal in on Sunday after-noons for activities not unconnected with playing cards'.

An Act for the Manchester Ship Canal Company to abandon the canal was passed at session in 1935/6. The canal could be filled in, but Manchester Corporation would be entitled at all times to have reasonable access to gas, electricity or water mains, cables and apparatus. The Ship Canal Company wanted to promote it as a development area of around 5 acres.

In a meeting between representatives of Manchester Corporation and the Ship Canal Company on 21 July 1939, the general manager of the canal company promoted the value of the disused canal arm by suggesting it could be used for a new seasoning technique of floating timber, or as a tip for excavations, or a storage area. The Corporation, who had another use for the tunnel in mind, informed the Ship Canal Company that they would prefer to rent it for five years with an option to purchase at the end of the period. Rental was agreed at £100 pa for five years, with the agreement that the Corporation would remove their works if they did not proceed with the sale. The Corporation agreed to pay for any damage caused during that period.

Memories of Manchester's Underground Canal

By Thomas Lloyd, Ex-River Inspector

Manchester's underground canal has been much in the public eye recently on account of its suggested suitability for ARP purposes. A few words now of its history and that of the surrounding district may be of interest.

The tunnel itself is in good condition and runs from under the Central Station Goods Yard, Deansgate and one side of Camp Street, to a point near Water Street called Brunswick Basin. It is cut out of rock and has a brick arch. The size of the tunnel is about 20ft by 16ft, the depth of waterway being 5ft, and a towpath for horses runs along one side.

Once in the early nineties I had occasion to bring out a sunken barge from under the goods station and we used a steam winch boat, fastening chains to the barge and pulling both boats about a hundred yards each time. During the operations the smoke from our boiler filled the tunnel and we had to kneel down with our mouths close to the floor of the boat in order to breathe. When we got the old barge out we broke her up, and put her on shore piece by piece.

Another time when the Manchester main drainage sewer was being placed along Deansgate and under the tunnel I was present at the fixing of the stop logs near the mouth of the tunnel at Grape Street. We had a large steam pump to draw off the water and when this was done we walked along the towpath under St John's Churchyard. About this point we saw many grey stalactites hanging from the walls and I took some home to my sister, telling her they were from the corpses in the graveyard.

While working under Deansgate we used Lucigen Lamps (Lucy Jones we called them) and once one went out. The man looking after them was a rough lump of a chap only happy in a fight, and when he was using the pricker in the burner the oil suddenly spurted out in his face and eyes. He screamed that he was blinded and we rushed him off to hospital - in a cab, for there were no motors in those days. Anyhow, he came back to work again next day, seeing as he said 'better than before.'

When the job was finished and the time came to pull out the stop logs the bottom one made of pitch-pine and measuring 14in x 7in jammed and I had to cut it in two at a depth of 4ft under water. We used specially made chisel bars 8ft long.

During the Great War a shaft was sunk to the tunnel just underneath the goods yard and a lift fixed to take railway wagons from the yard above to the barges below. This was to enable goods to be sent to and from the docks without carrying them across Manchester. The tunnel was widened for a length of 100ft under the goods yard so that the wagons could be lowered alongside the boats. In peace time the practice

continued overleaf

was found too expensive as the water had to be pumped from the Irwell to supply the Brunswick Basin, tunnel and locks. If the tunnel, which lies below the street surface at depths varying from a few feet to twenty-five feet was adopted for ARP purposes, it probably would require reinforcing with concrete and suitable entrances would have to be made at various points. The number of people it could shelter is estimated at anything between five and ten thousand, and I have heard fifteen thousand mentioned. It is about three-quarters of a mile in length.

The district all around the Brunswick Basin is called the Old Quay for navigation purposes and I remember a flat barge laden with cable drums taking a list and putting them all in the Basin. They weighed 2 to 3 tons each and it was my duty to lift them out with the salvage boat. Incidentally those were the first cable drums I ever saw. It was near this spot also that the barge Emma was launched and capsized as mentioned in the 'Manchester Man'. Once when we were blasting rock to give depth for the berthing of pleasure steamers using the Irwell to the Ship Canal we were in Brunswick Basin for some reason and one of our men put a canister of shot for a joke into a fire used for hooping wheels. It was dinner time and the terrific explosion brought out all Water Street, but the joker was not discovered.

My father was River Inspector before me and after each flood it was necessary to sound the fairway to give navigable draught to barges using the Irwell, and in the Seventies it was a real treat for me to sail with them down the river when this was being done. Then it was necessary for the dredger to clear mounds of silt that had accumulated. I have in my possession a silver salver in the shape of a lady's cupped hands that was dredged up near the Basin. The man who saw it come up with the buckets got hold of it before my father and he was well over ninety when he sent for me and gave me the salver with its history. I have had it now for about twenty-five years. It was supposed to have been part of the proceeds of a robbery which had been thrown into the river. During these dredgings lots of counterfeit coins were also dredged up.

The same men working on this job had each year to clean a feeder brook that ran from what is now Wilbraham Road Station to the Bridgewater Canal at Stretford. It was about the time of the noted burglar, Charles Peace, that they unearthed from the feeder-brook side a quantity of jewellery from another supposed robbery. The men were in clover until the police rounded them up and I never heard the final result.

Going back to the Irwell when passenger boats were plying from the Exchange Stage opposite the Cathedral to the newly opened Ship Canal, I remember during one of the floods a pile log came down and sank one of the steamers. I took the salvage boat to get her up and what an audience we had to watch the work. It was found necessary to turn her on one side, lift her bow, repair the hole, then put her straight and pump out all the water before taking her to Brunswick Basin where she lay some weeks before being taken to dock for repairs.

Brunswick Basin reaches from Quay Street to Grape Street and has many sunken barges lying there, it was bought over, along with the tunnel, by the Ship Canal Company in the Eighties.

● **From an article published in a company magazine. When Thomas Lloyd retired in 1981, he was the last of eight generations of his family to work on the canals. In recognition of this achievement, the Manchester Ship Canal Company, owners of Bridgewater Canal, renamed the bridge over the canal, at Oughtrington near Lymm, as the Lloyd Bridge.**

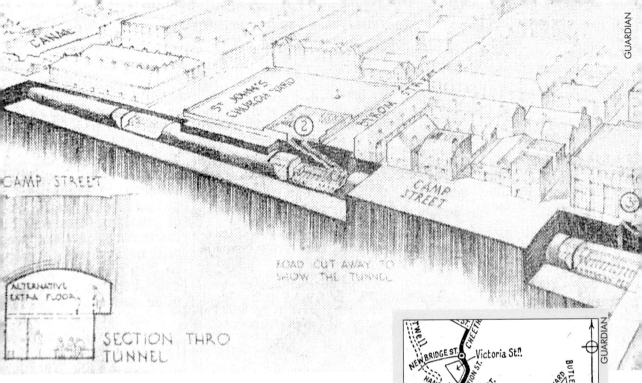

SECTION THRO TUNNEL

ALTERNATIVE EXTRA FLOOR.

Section through drawing of the canal shelter, intially showing three entrances, and the possibility of two tiers

AIR-RAID SHELTER

In the lead-up the last world war, this long-forgotten tunnel became the focus of attention. because on 3 February 1939 the ARP committee was considering the City Engineer's proposals for air-raid shelters in the Victoria Arches and the disused Manchester and Salford Junction Canal tunnel. The schemes had already been sent to the Home Office for approval. Initially, the plan had been to make the canal tunnel into a two-tier shelter.

By 22 June 1939, the Home Office had approved the use of Victoria Arches and 'the underground canal' as air-raid shelters. The canal scheme involved building a dam at one end and draining the 600 yard long tunnel. It would be divided into 16 chambers by reinforced bulkhead walls. Four entrances were planned, but the Home Office stipulated a further two should be made.

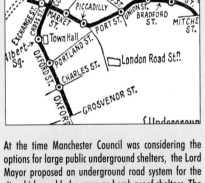

At the time Manchester Council was considering the options for large public underground shelters, the Lord Mayor proposed an underground road system for the city which would also serve as bomb proof shelters. The scheme would ease traffic congestion with eleven entry points going down 80ft, a spiral ramp 10 ft wide and two tunnels running approximately north, south, east and west.

The City Engineer's response highlighted the difficulties with the scheme. The tunnels would have been 30ft wide for buses and traffic in both directions, and run under roads to reduce negotiation with land owners. The sloping entrances to the tunnel would be 70ft long, and there would be an expensive system of ventilation. The scheme would take three years and cost £2 million.

The City Engineer also suggested alternative underground bomb proof accommodation for 50,000 people for around £450,000, which could later be adapted into the road system. The time required to plan and construct any of these systems plus the immense cost meant that all the ideas were deferred by the council.

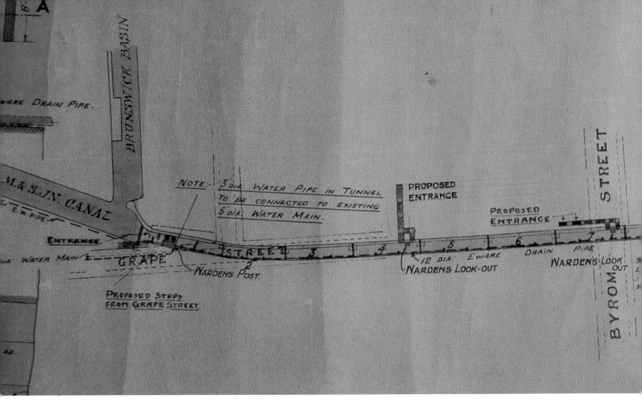

Above: Plan to show how the tunnel would have blast walls for added protection, and the provision of warden and first aid posts

Below: The ARP Committee about to enter the canal tunnel

On 9 August 1939 members of the Air Raid Precautions Committee inspected eight types of shelters in the city including Victoria Arches and the canal tunnel. It was envisaged that the two large shelters would also be used to store ambulance equipment, gas masks and provisions. The canal tunnel clearly required a lot of cleaning-up to make it habitable:

'CLEANSING NEEDED

The members of the committee, corporation and police officials saw it in its present damp and dirty state, and the bubbles coming slimily to the surface of the water suggested that a lot of cleaning will be necessary after the water is run out. But there was in the dank air of the tunnel a feeling of security and a sense of deep

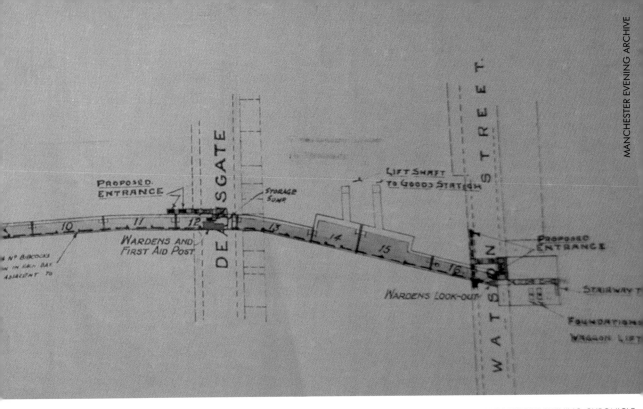

MANCHESTER EVENING ARCHIVE

MANCHESTER EVENING CHRONICLE

protection which did more than any argument to discount the 'official' desire for shelters in which the population can be deployed rather than concentrated.'

(Guardian 10 Aug 1939)

Following instructions to begin construction, draining the canal in the tunnel began on Monday 25 August and finished five days later. The mud then had to be cleared. The ARP committee had been originally told the water could be drained in one hour! Over a million gallons of water had to be drained out and around 4000 cubic yards of silt removed before the bed could be laid with concrete. A 35-ft wide dam was built to prevent the encroachment of water at the tunnel entrance. The work to modify the tunnel into an air-raid shelter was carried out by Wellerman Brothers of Sheffield for £25,836 2s 0d. The Ship Canal Company charged £2000 for the use of the Canal arm, although this may have been reduced because of the reduced liabilities.

Clearing out the tons of silt from the canal bed

Overleaf: The derelict transshipment dock prior to draining the tunnel

197

The shelter is completed

Seating

In August 1940, the Manchester Emergency Committee received instructions from the Ministry of Home Security that seating had to be supplied in all public shelters.

By September 1940, the shelter was open day and night. It was reported that over 100 people were sleeping there each night. They took their own bedding and were accommodated in one huge bay, presumably the old transshipment dock. The heads of the wooden plank beds were positioned next to the old canal tow path. Hot water to make tea was obtainable from one of the five wardens' posts. One lady told a reporter about how much they enjoyed the midnight tea parties, which she described as a 'grand do'.

midnight tea parties ... a 'grand do'.

Four generators powered the air-conditioning system, drawing in fresh air from stacks 40 ft above ground. Because of the shortages of timber, seating was provided using benches and collapsible wooden chairs from the parks. There had been complaints of misbehaviour in shelters in September 1940, but a tour by a divisional warden came to the conclusion that the complaints had been exaggerated.

Bunk beds

It quickly became evident that the authorities needed to take action regarding the provision of bunks and further measures on ventilation and hygiene. Councillor Harper, the central divisional warden, reported that people were travelling long distances to go to shelters, carrying mattresses and bedding. It was announced in October 1940, following a meeting of Manchester's Emergency Committee, that three-tiered bunks with water-proof mattresses would be provided for 36,000 people.

The new bunks

Disinfection

Emergency doors were left open by wardens to provide more ventilation but, as one of them commented, '...the atmosphere in the shelters by 4am generally speaking is poor. Some of my wardens at their own expense have brought disinfectant sprays which they use frequently in their shelters, but this method is only temporary, and a systematic method of disinfection is required'.

By December 1940, the authorities were preparing to disinfect both the Victoria Arches and the canal tunnel and would be providing the services of a doctor and nurse. Also it had been decided that paid marshals or stewards could be employed at a ratio of two per 500 persons.

'Shelter unsafe'

Lord Horder, on a visit to shelters in Liverpool and Manchester in January 1941, was not impressed by the canal shelter. He said '...you have got a shelter... of which, quite frankly, I can hardly believe that the authorities will not take the view that some parts can never be hygienically conditioned so as to be safe. I have ventured to suggest for the safety of Manchester citizens that parts of the shelter should be disallowed'.

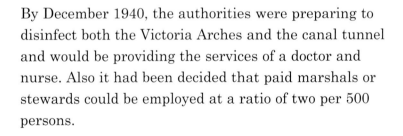

'...you have got a shelter... some parts can never be hygienically conditioned so as to be safe.'

Present day bricked off entrance

Sir Norton Barclay, chairman of the Manchester Emergency Committee, announced afterwards that, subject to the agreement of the Regional Commissioner, they would begin improvements to remedy the dampness problems by installing a false roof and walling to the damp sections of the tunnel. Also, a canteen, bunks, a sickbay and heating were to be provided.

In January 1941 because of the popularity of the larger shelters, the Emergency Committee decided to begin a ticket admission system to the canal arm shelter, so that people living in the neighbourhood could reserve places. It was reported that up to 300 people - mostly women and children - were using the shelter. They had taken their own beds there and had sectioned the tunnel space into small dormitories.

Scarlet fever

On 14 January 1941 newspapers reported four cases of scarlet fever in the tunnel shelter. Four children were taken to Monsall Isolation Hospital, and the tunnel was sealed, while the sick bay was disinfected, and the rest of the tunnel fumigated in readiness for public use later that evening.

The authorities were confident that these were isolated cases and that there was no danger of an epidemic. There was no evidence of shelter life increasing infectious diseases in the city. Records showed over the past year that such cases were unusually low. Only thirty scarlet fever cases were being treated at Monsall Hospital, where there was capacity for one hundred and eighty.

By March 22 1941, work was under way to provide 1200 steel or wooden bunks in the tunnel. They were to be three-tiered and would resemble the accommodation found in 'an American sleeping-car'. The bunks were 5ft

SCARLET FEVER CASES IN SHELTER

—BUT NO FEAR OF EPIDEMIC

MANCHESTER medical authorities do not take a serious view of an outbreak of scarlet fever discovered in one of the city's underground air raid shelters.

Four children removed from the shelter to Monsall Isolation Hospital were to-day stated to have scarlet fever, but there is no fear of an epidemic.

The shelter was sealed, and it will be disinfected and fumigated in readiness for use to-night.

The Emergency Committee, which met this afternoon to discuss among other matters the strengthening of basements in city premises to augment shelter accommodation, was expected to

6in long and 2ft wide and constructed so that 'even the most restless sleeper would not roll out'. Timber from houses demolished by bombs was used to construct the wooden version which would cost 30s to make. The steel version would cost 45s. The bottoms of the bunks had either wire netting or hessian beneath the mattresses. Cabin ladders were to be provided for the top bunk. The authorities made it clear that the public would not be allowed to reserve particular bunks.

Manchester's version of the bunks

Manchester received 39,000 bunks for its shelters, slightly adapted from the Government's design by the City Architect, Noel Hill and tested by the Chief Constable and members of the Emergency Committee.

Because of comments about the dampness in the shelter, a false roof was put in and the walls lined where water percolated through the bare rock. More toilets were to be installed with exhaust fans nearby. A canteen was provided serving light refreshments and run by voluntary organisations on a non-profit making basis. A sick bay was already available.

Ear plugs

Ear plugs to help a peaceful night's sleep were also to be distributed. The plugs were issued in pairs at one size - one-inch long hollow brown pliable rubber, with a rim so that they could be fastened together with string. Wardens who issued them would advise on snipping off the end in order to fit into the ear. The plug resembled the shape of a miniature ninepin. Some were distributed door-to-door by Air-Raid Wardens.

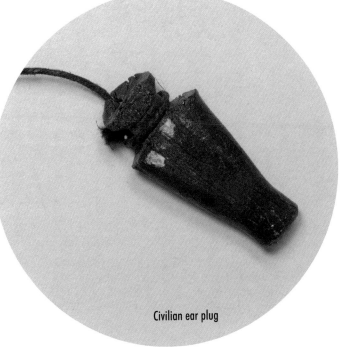

Civilian ear plug

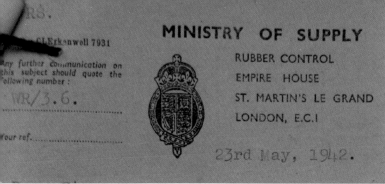

They had been originally requested by the Army to help cushion the noise from screaming bombs and guns, and it was thought they would help civilians to endure the frightening noise of bombing in their shelters. Home Office literature stated: *'When worn, the plugs do not seriously interfere with the hearing of ordinary speech, etc, but they do reduce the crash and concussion of explosions. Their object is not so much to obviate physical damage to the ear as to prevent the shattering effect of noise on the nerves.'* 45 million pairs of ear plugs were produced, and those surplus to requirements were passed back to the Rubber Controller because of the shortage of rubber.

Other health measures discussed were communal gargles, spraying of shelters during the night, and daily washing with strong disinfectant. Medical officers would tour the shelters every night, and everyone with infectious colds and complaints would be examined. There was also discussion of providing germ (or anti-infection) masks made of cellulose acetate, five and half inches square. Alternatively four layers of muslin could be used.

Improvements

By October 1941 the conditions in both the Arches and the tunnel had greatly improved. One newspaper reported 'The two large subterranean shelters in the city have been improved out of all recognition, and will be models of their kind in a few weeks, when the finishing touches have been added. In one, (the tunnel?) where water dripped continuously for a year, now false steel roofs carry the water into drainage channels, and a combined electric heating and ventilation plan with thermostatic control, is already in action. Both have canteens with electric kitchens, several boilers, well-

Lillian Doherty (née Carter) has memories of MSJC tunnel. She went into the shelter via the entrances at Grape Street and Lower Byrom Street.

She lived in Water Street and was thirteen at the height of the bombing. Lillian remembered two lads being killed after they picked up incendiary bombs.

She had to stay in the bunk beds built along the tunnel walls, but she really wanted to explore the other bays. Her parents told her to lie down and go to sleep, but she was frightened by the sound of the bombs. Adults had to sleep on the floor of the tunnel. The shelter was packed, and included members of the forces on leave.

Although some of the surrounding streets were severely damaged by the bombing, the homes on Lower Byrom Street did not even suffer a cracked window pane.

After the war, she and her younger sister found the steps down into the tunnel and went down with candles. Many local children had found this way in.

equipped medical posts, numerous water closets, drinking fountains, and washing bowls with hot and cold water. One even has a rest-room, with book-shelves, for the staff. Between them they have bunks for over 1300 people each allocated to a ticket-holder. The walls are distempered a pleasant cream'.

It had taken nearly two years to make the shelters reasonably hospitable and to impose rules of behaviour. Signs in the tunnel prohibited tea leaves being poured into the wash basins, but were to be emptied into the bins provided. Also, all bedding had to be removed by 9am each day so that the shelter could be disinfected.

With the ending of the war, the shelters were officially closed in May 1945 by the Ministry of Home Security.

Canal sold

The main section of the canal, from Rochdale Canal up to the Granada Studio property, was sold by Manchester Ship Canal Company to the Heron Corporation Ltd (Garrard Securities) in 1977. Granada had purchased their part of the canal in 1955.

Regional Defence survey

In 1951 the Ministry of Works began a survey of accommodation to be used in an emergency on behalf of the Regional Civil Defence. The Home Office gave priority to the underground air-raid shelters acquired by local authorities and used during the last war. The schedule for the old canal tunnel described as the 'Canal Arm Shelter' indicated that it was owned by the Manchester Ship Canal Company and that it accommodated 783 (bunked) and 585 (seated) - total 1368 persons. The shelter had been dismantled and the entrances built up, but the masonry work had not been touched.

Surviving shelter toilet

Overleaf: A rare war-time photograph of the canal tunnel in use as a shelter. Park benches taken down there can be seen next to the old towpath on the left hand side.

PEPPERFOTO/GETTY IMAGES

Eastern tunnel portal with the warden look-out post. The framing on the wall probably supported a shelter notice.

The report stated the tunnel had been used between 1918 and 1938 to accommodate barges under repair. There were four entrances specially built at street level, with one entrance in a yard at canal level, which was previously a dry dock and now filled in to form a road transport yard.

Approximately three quarters of the tunnel was regarded as usable. The remaining section in Bays 8-11 had a 'very objectionable odour', the source unknown. During the outbreak of fever these bays were put out of use. The brick arches were in good condition, but the roof was very damp in three or four places, with dripping water in Bay 7 under Byrom Street. The tunnel was 80% brick-lined, with the remainder trimmed rock face.

The tunnel was cut out of soft bunter sandstone, and the report author, EA Oliver, is definite regarding the building method; '...there can be no doubt that it was constructed by the 'cut and cover' method' so the cover over the canal would be a 'fill' and not virgin rock.'

Rather frighteningly, he thought that although the tunnel (apart from Bays 1 and 2) would provide sufficient protection against HE bombs, casualties would be expect-ed from a direct hit by the larger 500lb MC bombs. The total cost of adapting the tunnel was estimated at £35,000.

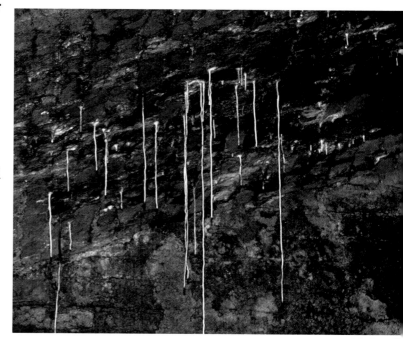

The canal tunnel today is a fascinating reminder of the enterprise of the canal company to construct a route and a tunnel right into the heart of the city, and also the dark days of the last World War when people got on with their lives in sometimes difficult and dangerous conditions. The transshipment dock, wagon hoist and the hoist shafts are to be seen, as are the extensive workings of the war-time shelter such as war-den's lookouts, first-aid posts, toilet booths and even a few notices and signs. There have been plans in the past to make this impressive underground area into a public visitor attraction. It is to be hoped that they will be implemented so that everyone can experience the atmosphere and sights of this amazing tunnel for themselves .

Opposite top left: Evidence of temporary roof structures above the tunnel arch, erected because of water dripping onto people in the shelter

Opposite below left: War-time brick cubicles and an old post for tying up the canal boats

Left: Two wagon hoists from the canal to the Central Station goods yard

Below: One of the two passage ways from the transshipment dock to to the warehouse hoists

Above: Arching supporting the buildings in the Central Station goods yard

Opposite top: The towpath and the protected way through the blast wall at the back

Left: Immediately below Deansgate. The first-aid post on the left had separate sections for males and females. Water has percolated back into this section of the tunnel towards the eastern end, because the floor level is lower.

'Guardian'

Opposite top left: The 'safeguarding' map indicating the properties under which Guardian would pass.

Opposite top right: Voice frequency telegraph equipment and test desks in London

Opposite below: Shaft-head machinery in the centre of Manchester during the construction of Guardian

Guardian was part of a chain of underground workings with London (Kingsway) and Birmingham (Anchor). The system connected with a transatlantic cable to the USA via the repeater station at Oban, Scotland, and with mainland Europe under the Channel at St Margaret's Bay, Kent. Their purpose was to preserve national telephone communications in the event of an enemy attack, even if the buildings above were flattened.

Guardian was the smallest of the city-based terminal and switching centres. There were plans for a fourth centre in Glasgow but after initial ground testing this was abandoned. The cost of building the three exchanges for the Post Office was £4,600,000 - the original estimate had been £6,400,000. The costings did not include the telephone equipment, but as this was a defence system it qualified for NATO funding.

Guardian's central complex lay between Dickenson Street and York Street with a tunnel to Dial House, Salford, under the River Irwell, and two exit tunnels at Lockton Close, Ardwick and Islington Street Salford.

GOVERNMENT PLANS

From the once 'top-secret' Government documents much is revealed about the process of building the tunnels and of the efforts to keep details of the workings away from public and media attention. It had been hoped to submit the Post Office Works Bill during the Parliamentary session of 1957/8 but because the Book of Reference could not be finished in time, the Bill was submitted during the following session 1958/59. The Bill was to enable defence

regulations of land to be rescinded, and provide the Postmaster General with the necessary powers to maintain the communication systems in deep tunnels and in the three larger excavations in London, Birmingham and Manchester.

The Book of Reference was a statutory requirement consisting of a list of properties under which the tunnels passed and the particulars of owners, lessees and occupiers, together with the local councils affected.

Guardian was part of a national network of communications put together after the Second World War under top secret plans entitled 'The Machinery of Government in War'.

It was being completed at the time of the escalating tension in the Cold War period, between communist nations and the democratic free world. People in government thought that there would be a limited nuclear strike by the Soviets backed up by a land invasion after three months when the radiation threat had diminished. Soviet maps in the Ryland's Library collection, showing Manchester tank routes, indicate the seriousness of the threat.

This would have given the British government around six weeks to make Guardian into an operational bunker. A 'war room' had been set up and there was limited accommodation and food for both telephone staff and others.

The development of nuclear missiles meant that Guardian had less strategic importance and although it was maintained as an exchange, its time as a top secret installation came to an end.

It would be used as a basis for giving notice to those affected by the Bill. Mr W Williams and Mr S D Mellor were the Manchester Post Office employee contacts for the preparation of the Book of Reference.

The book with its associated plans was prepared by the Ministry of Works, and usually took at least six months. As this was required by 20th November, it was considered too short a notice. A report dated 26 August 1957 stated the end of February as the revised target date. There was no question of streamlining the procedure because the book had to be meticulously prepared.

This did not affect the Post Office, who were safeguarded by a clause in the 1945 Requisitioned Land and War Works Act, which allowed two further years to December 1957 after the expiration of emergency defence regultions. It was also expected to be extended until December 1958. This 1956 document summarises the situation at that time:

'...We are agreed that it would be improvident not to obtain additional limited powers required for the maintenance to the extent necessary, of systems which are already in existence and in which much public money has been sunk.

...The communication system includes, in addition to surface works, three large 'shelters' about one hundred feet below ground, at Chancery Lane and underneath Birmingham and Manchester in which telephone equipment for trunk lines is placed, together with considerable accommodation for personnel. These shelters are connected to points elsewhere by cables in so-called 'deep tunnels'. It is understood that the equipment in these excavations is now used as an integral part of the normal peace-time telephone system.'

216

LAND ACQUISITION
AT ARDWICK AND SALFORD

By the time the revised Bill came to Parliament, all the acquisitions of surface sites relating to the tunnels had been made. Over 400 surface property owners above the deep chambers had been approached during a nine month period in connection with the Book of Reference. None had objected. By April 1958, a contract between the owners and the Post Office had been agreed for the 20/34 Russell Street site, Ardwick, after the site was requisitioned in December 1954. The transaction was delayed by chief rent problems. The Post Office erected a shafthead on the site, where there was to be a ventilation shaft 4ft 6 in wide and 6ft high. At Islington Street, Salford, the site had been requisitioned in 1951. The two sites were not mentioned in the Bill because neither was regarded as having direct access to the equipment tunnels. The report then refers to other un-named shafts: 'It was subsequently confirmed there were other shafts giving direct access to the Manchester Equipment tunnels ...'

Site 7A, Russell Street, Ardwick, January 1955 - the southern exit of Guardian in the event of a direct hit on central Manchester

SECRECY

On the instruction of the security services, the Post Office did not wish to make known the depths of the underground chambers. Presumably, Government security services were aware that the latest enemy bombs would have penetrated the tunnel and therefore the tunnels were extremely vulnerable. Consultants had advised that buildings in Manchester could have foundations to a depth of 50ft without risking damage to themselves or the tunnels. It was thought necessary that building plans should be examined in case of risk. There were to be no restrictions on the rights of owners to build on land above the tunnels, but local planning authorities were request-ed to consult with the Ministry of Works where new developments might infringe on the works below.

(1) What is the purpose of these tunnels?

Initially it would perhaps be well to stick to the formula suggested in the draft speech that these tunnels are used for essential Post Office purposes.

The real function of these works is set out in brief 3. It would however, be undesirable on security grounds to reveal as much as this. If pressed on what they are for, something on the following lines might suffice:-

"As there is a security aspect to the works covered by this Bill, your Lordships would not wish — nor expect — me to go into detail about their precise function. I can, however, say that they contain equipment essential to the national communications system, particularly in the event of war".

Advice on what to reveal publically about the true function of the tunnels in the House of Lords debate on the Post Office Works Bill

A memo regarding the 'nature and purpose of the works', stated that *'for security reasons we do not wish to make public the size or depth of the chambers or the purposes for which they are required..'* The main chambers in the Post Office Bill were described as 'up to thirty feet in diameter' linking with smaller tunnels and contained ' transmission and switching equipment which it would be desirable to try to safe-guard in war, to assist in maintaining vital long-distance communications... The equipment chambers vary in depth from 60 to 90ft below the surface to which they are connected by shafts for ventilation, lifts and other services. These shafts all terminate in property which the Post Office owns or in which it has acquired an interest.' The equipment chambers were joined to main cable routes on the perimeters of the cities. These routes were described as 'deep lines' and were not in the Bill.

, Salford	Access Cables	7'0"	P.O. freehold	Permanently	Subway to Telephone House plus manhole in shafthead	Cable	
		–	Extended tenancy	Temporarily			Used by contractor for working space. Probably to be given up by June 1957.
rk St. George St. nchester	Personnel access Ventilation, lift, Cables, Services	18'0"	P.O. freehold	Permanently	Subway to Central Exchange. plus manhole in shafthead that will be suspended by normal P.O. building.	Apparatus	
		–	3 leases expiring 24.6.57	Temporarily	–	–	ditto
rge St. chester	Goods Access Ventilation, Crane, Services	22'0" – 23'2½"	P.O. freehold	Permanently	Shafthead & special surface building with staircase	Apparatus	
t. Ardwick, ester	Access Cables	12'0"	Requisitioned 18.12.54 (DR51)	Permanently	Manhole	Cable	Negotiations proceeding for purchase of freehold.
		–	Requisitioned 18.12.54 converted to 2 year tenancy and now extended to 24.6.57.	Temporarily	–	–	Used by contractor for working spare. Probably to be given up by June 1957.

The Government was liable for any surface damage from subsidence due to deep chambers falling in or not being kept water-tight. Government officials recalled cracks appearing in the buildings belonging to the Prudential Insurance Company, at Staple Inn, Chancery Lane, London, during construction of extensions of Post Office tunnels in 1951. The tunnels were originally constructed for military purposes during WW2 but were taken over by the Post Office and extended between 1951 and 1956. The company blamed the damage on the works although this was never proven. The Government, anxious not make public what was happening underground, reached a compromise out-of-court settlement of £7000. A contingency fund of £35,000 a year was held to cover maintenance costs.

Internal document with details of the Manchester and Salford workings (Page 2 overleaf)

MANCHESTER NOT INFORMED

It was clear that the relevant local authorities were not given details about the workings when there were enquiries from Manchester and Birmingham Corporations for information including depths of the tunnels. It was explained that this could not be given for security reasons

Iron rings of cable tunnel,
September 1954

and that the only advice they could give was that the workings were more than 60ft below ground.

Prior to the debate on the Bill in the House of Lords, guidance was given on how to answer questions regarding the purpose of the tunnels. *'Initially it would perhaps be well to stick to the formula suggested in the draft speech that these tunnels are used for essential Post Office purposes. The real function of these works is set out in brief 3. It would, however, be undesirable on security grounds to reveal as much as this. If pressed on what they are for, something on the following lines might suffice: 'As there is a security aspect to the works covered by this Bill, your Lordships would not wish - nor expect - me to go into detail about their precise function. I can however, say that they contain equipment essential to our communication systems'.*

The decision not to reveal the depth of the tunnels on security grounds was made in 1957. It was put to the test when the Manchester Evening News and the Birmingham Post both enquired about visits to the tunnels in order to publish articles. They were given some encouragement by Admiral Thompson that permission may be granted, but after further internal discussions and advice from the security authorities, it was agreed that 'it would be dangerous to depart from the policy which had been laid down...'. The press were to be told to 'exercise discretion in seeking information on defence matters'.

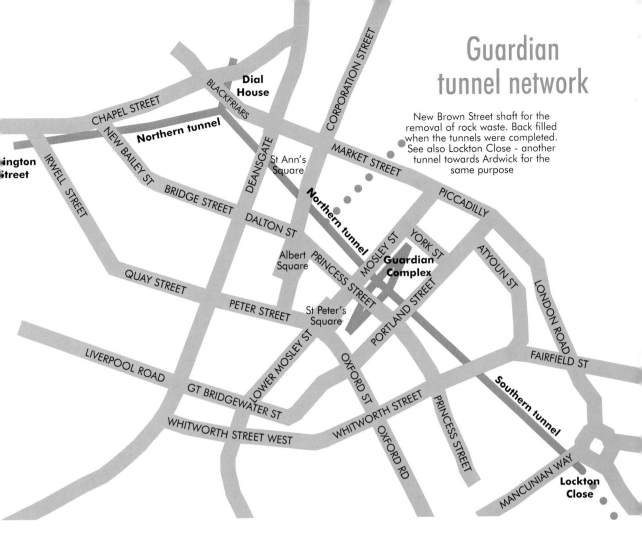

Guardian tunnel network

New Brown Street shaft for the removal of rock waste. Back filled when the tunnels were completed. See also Lockton Close - another tunnel towards Ardwick for the same purpose

Internal document of the Manchester and Salford workings

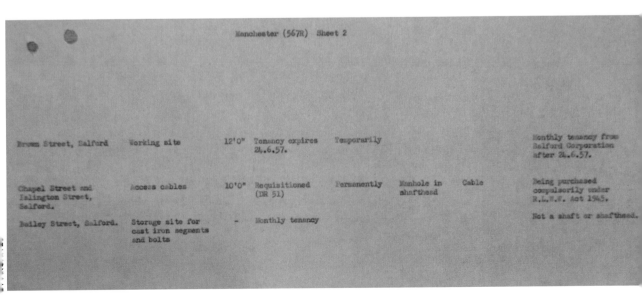

Manchester (567R) Sheet 2

Brown Street, Salford	Working site	12'0"	Tenancy expires 24.6.57.	Temporarily			Monthly tenancy from Salford Corporation after 24.6.57.
Chapel Street and Islington Street, Salford.	Access cables	10'0"	Requisitioned (DR 51)	Permanently	Manhole in shafthead	Cable	Being purchased compulsorily under R.L.N.W. Act 1945.
Bailey Street, Salford.	Storage site for cast iron segments and bolts	-	Monthly tenancy				Not a shaft or shafthead.

221

'BEST KEPT SECRET'

The underground telephone exchanges were made public on 7 June 1968 with the withdrawal of 'D' (Defence) Notices. Mr John Stonehouse, the Postmaster General, on a visit to the former top secret establishment in Manchester in October of that year, said it had been 'the best kept secret in Manchester ... for the past ten years'. He stated that telephone systems had been placed deep underground both to avoid 'serious sub-congestion in cities' and to protect the telephone service from 'total breakdown in a severe emergency'. The truth, however, was that it had long been known that improved enemy bombs would have penetrated the tunnels. It had originally been built to withstand a 20-kiloton atomic bomb but by 1955 this had been superseded by the new Soviet H-bomb, known then as 'Penza-9'. The only thing being protected by then was government from the embarrassment of continuing with a project that was obsolete and had cost so much money to build and maintain.

It is interesting to note that during Mr Stonehouse's visit to Manchester on 8 October, a GPO spokesman said there was a similar exchange in Glasgow. Yet by 22 October, the Minister revealed in Parliament that the Scottish exchange had never been built. It is thought, however, that there was an underground BT installation in Glasgow which served an east coast cable route.

Ventilation shaft and surface building close to completion, November 1960

GUARDIAN DETAILS

Former confidential documents reveal other details: the Manchester and Birmingham tunnels were made of concrete, with treated casing up to 2ft thick to prevent water seepage. The tunnels were mainly of horse-shoe construction. There was accommodation for 35 engineering maintenance staff, compared to 140 in London and 60 in Birmingham.

In an internal note dated 16 May 1958 before the revised Bill was submitted, consultants advised that no excavations of buildings should approach within 30 feet of the internal surface of any tunnel lining. Also that 'the crown loading due to any future surface construction should not impose a total distributed load on the surface of the tunnel lining of more than 6 tons per square foot'.

There seemed relatively little risk from building operations in Manchester, with a minimum depth of cover of 60ft. The tunnels were constructed in solid rock-bunter sandstone - 'a reddish brown pervious sandstone of fine medium grain with intervening bands of impervious sillstone and occasional bands of pebbly sandstone.'.

Guardian's main central section containing welfare, ventilation and access tunnels was approximately 820 yards long, with further cable tunnels - to Ardwick 1004 yards, and Salford with a spur to Dial House 1895 yards. Unlike the other centres Guardian was connected to local authority sewers.

Jimmy Hodgkinson (water services engineer - a good welder) made the tunnel model out of pipes. The model gave visitors a good appreciation of the complex in relation to the streets above.

Jimmy later died from natural causes while at work in Guardian.

Above: Site 6, George Street, Manchester, March 1956

Opposite: Site 4, Chapel Street, Salford, March 1956

TUNNEL CONSTRUCTION

It took three years to build, beginning in 1953. Nuttall's, the contractors, had been founded in 1865 by James Nuttall, based at Burlington Street, Manchester, working on roads and sewers. Under the leadership of his son Edmund, the company had developed into a major international business working on many notable projects including the Liver Building, Mersey Tunnel and the Haweswater Aqueduct. They would go on later to be one of the main contractors of the Channel Tunnel. Some of the workers on the site in central Manchester suffered infections in open cuts, thought to have been caused by digging into the the site where plague victims were buried. It was claimed that the ground was still infected.

The first Post Office staff had to be lowered in a cage into a hole in the ground to get to work, by means of one of the contractor cranes, before the stairs were built.

225

Although there may have been parts of the system where no explosives could be used due to the danger of bringing more water into the tunnels, eye-witnesses down there remembered loud thuds and excavated material falling into the water.

There were seven surface work-sites: Site 4 - Chapel Street, Salford; Site 5 - York Street and George Street, Manchester; Site 6 - 49-55 George Street, Manchester; Site 7A - Russell Street, Ardwick, Site 11 - Brown Street Salford; Site 12 - Chapel Street/Islington Street Salford; Site 13 - Bailey Street, Salford. It is not clear why there is a gap in the numbered sites between 8 and 10, but it is known there were two extensions to the system at New Brown Street, and in Ardwick which were later back-filled after construction.

Opposite top: Site 11 Brown Street, Salford March 1956. On the left is the 'muck gantry' and shaft head gear. The concreting plant and pump are in the centre, and to the right the top of the winch house.

Opposite below: Site 12, Chapel Street, March 1956

Below left: Site 11, Brown Street, c1954

Below: Brown Street January 1954

227

THE TUNNEL WORKERS

Ironically, it is claimed the tunnellers, at the height of the 'Cold War', were using Russian-made equipment. The excavated material from 'Guardian' was taken away by lorries in the middle of the night and deposited on the banks of the river Mersey around south Manchester to build up the flood barriers.

Mike Russell was one of the tunnellers in the 'Dilly' and he remembers the work and his mates with great affection and pride. He was one of the 'tramps' who would go around the country to work on tunnels and other large civil engineering projects. They were known by their nick-names - Mike was 'Mad Tip' (he was from Tipperary). Then there were his close mates - 'Monkey O'Brien' (the explosives man), 'Mad Hagerty', and 'Tramp Mackenzie'. They preferred to live in large camps where there would be a post office, nissen huts, games room, and either a

Final jointing in the southern cable tube, April 1956

Concrete mixer and pump in the northern cable tube, January 1956

'dry canteen', or 'wet' serving alcohol. In the better camps, they had their own rooms. At other times they would live in 'digs'. Mike remembered 'the death cell' in Warner Street, Moss Side run by a female former Strangeways prison warder, where they shared a room heated only by a stove gas ring. They could have been 'gassed' because it was windowless and there was no ventilation. The beds were used day and night as they worked shifts, which caused problems at weekends when everyone was around.

Above: Attaching mesh and canvas to the wall of the southern cable tube to divert water, August 1955

Opposite: Concreting of arch and excavation of sump in Apparatus Tunnel 3, January 1956

Tunnellers worked hard in dangerous conditions. They worked eight-hour shifts and would often do a further four hours overtime. Their basic pay of 2s 6d an hour was supplemented by 5s yardage bonus for the number of rings or arches they put in. Mike was one of the four machine-men or drillers in his gang using Atlas air leg machines with the 'Leading Miner' in overall charge. Health and safety standards were different then, and to ask for ear protection would be risking dismissal.

They earned comparatively good money - 'poke'- and after being paid, they would go around the city 'well-hipped' and drink and gamble it away. There are no official details of worker injuries or deaths and Mike did not remember any serious incidents while he was working there. He did, however, recall the death of the winding gear operator, who was mugged outside a pub on Oldham Street.

Mike worked on the 'Dilly' for two periods. The first lasted about a year until he was sacked - for sending his girl-friend down the Guardian workings. He had been asked to take over the winding gear when the cage-man had not turned up for work. Mike went across to tell his wife-to-be, who worked at a nearby cafe, that he would not be seeing her that day because of his work duties. She persuaded him to show her what it was like in the tunnel, so against his better judgment while the boss was away, he lowered her and a friend down the 182ft shaft. He told them there was to be no 'screaming for Micky when you're down there.' While he was deciding whether it was safe to bring them back up from the pitch black tunnel, the manager, Mr Hill, returned and demanded that the cage was raised back to the top. Mike, realising he was in big trouble, tried to stall him but his boss insisted he brought it back up. The cage was raised for Mr Hill, with the sight of the two frightened girls clinging to each other. Mike pretended not to know who they were or who had sent them down there, until his girl friend blurted out 'Micky, it's dark down there!' The leading miner was sent for and Mike was immediately removed from the site. He was then 24 years old, and despite his misdemeanours he later returned to Manchester to work on the 'Dilly' tunnels to Ardwick and Salford. The Russell family were to have a further connection with Guardian because his son, also called Mike, went on to become manager of Guardian in the 1980s.

Contrary to what has been said, the tunnellers did know at the time that they were building a bomb-proof tunnel. According to Mike, Polish workers only made up approximately a quarter of the work-force; the majority of the rest were Irish. It has been stated that Poles were employed because they would not divulge anything about the top-secret site, because they did not speak English. This was not true, they spoke and understood the

233

language, and were perhaps more responsible than others with their money. As one Polish worker told Mike, 'when we get paid, we throw away the wage packet and keep the money, but you keep the wage packet and throw away the money!'

The furnishing of the tunnels was substantially completed by February 1957, although technicians involved in early testing of equipment recall that builders were still around filling leaks in the walls and that the conditions were grim, with lots of running water. Records have never been made public about worker casualties, which there surely were in such a dangerous environ-ment. The only known incident was the death, in the 1960s, of a construction worker who fell down a shaft during the building of the Rutherford Exchange on George Street. Staff at Guardian heard a loud noise but did not realise what it was. The accident is thought to have happened on a Friday, and the police were at Guardian the following Monday, after it had been reported that the worker had not returned home and his motor bike had remained in the yard over the weekend. The Police searched the complex and found the worker's body at the bottom of the shaft. The man had only recently been married.

It seems odd today that the public did not question more the strange sight of shaft head machinery in the centre of the city on what became the site for the Piccadilly Plaza. They accepted that it was simply a Post Office working. Details were not made public, which would surely have made people more curious. An engineer, with no connection to the project, has told me how he calculated the depth of the mysterious workings by noting how many times the wheel turned.

234

EXCHANGE OPENED

Equipment installation of the new automatic trunk network for the region began in August 1957, and with staff working through the night, Guardian trunk non-director exchange opened for traffic at 8am on 7 December 1958. 'Pioneer', a larger unit, was brought into service between November and December 1959.

Below: Northern cable tunnel April 1958, and the test desk

Improvements in the system continued with the opening of a new STD system at the Rutherford Exchange in 1967 at a cost of £600,000. Before, most of the STD traffic had passed through the Pioneer Exchange at Dial House, Salford. In 1970 Turret in Salford opened, which dealt with dialled trunk calls from 26 of the 46 exchanges around Manchester, passing them either by cable or through the microwave radio network to the communications towers at Heaton Park and at Sutton, Macclesfield .

FEATURES OF THE TUNNELS

In a Manchester Evening News article entitled 'The Truth about Manchester's 'nuclear bunker', March 1983, the reporter sought to dispel some of the myths that continue to the present day. He found no evidence of fall-out suits or anything else which would indicate that Guardian was a nuclear holocaust nerve centre. Instead, Michael Duffy found a deserted canteen with an aquarium of tropical fish. Next door was a mess room containing an old piano and indications of a recent game of pool. This was not the haven of the favoured few, but simply an outdated remnant of the Cold War. Guardian was one of several

MANCHESTER EVENING NEWS

Below top: Battery Room, lower level. It also had a stillage for producing distilled water for topping up the acid level in the battery cells. Customs and Excise periodically inspected it, to ensure it was not being used to produce whisky.

Below: Recreation room

ageing communications centres up and down the country. As a member of staff told him, 'maybe someone knows more than we do, but as far as we are concerned, this is just an underground telephone exchange'. Mr Duffy was given a guided tour of the main 1000ft tunnel, the cable-carrying 'tubes' to Salford and Ardwick, the artesian well, the accommodation and supplies for the engineers who would be besieged there in time of crisis. He also saw the heavy concrete doors which would shut in an emergency.

THE LOWER-LEVEL TUNNEL

The first room along the corridor was the power maintenance office, followed by the First Aid and then the rest/dining room. At one end of the oblong room, illuminated by fluorescent lighting, was a painting and at the other end there was a large tropical fish tank. Mirrors on the walls enhanced the lighting and sense of space. There were tables and chairs for the engineers' lunch and tea breaks. It would be crowded when the shift rota was in operation, especially the day shift.

The next room was the kitchen, and then the gents' toilet and washroom, recreation room, ladies' toilet, sewage ejection room, war room and cloakroom.

The sewage ejection room had pressure vessels, waste collection vessels and compressors. There was another fish tank here containing the fish who had been segregated from the tank in the rest room because of their tendency to eat the other fish!

A safe in the war room contained a manual with instructions for the manager on the operation of Guardian in an emergency. The safe could only be opened with a special code. There was a locker with pickaxes and shovels. On the wall was a map of the northwest with a cables overlay. The manual and maps were removed by BT head office after Guardian came off the Official Secrets Act. A speaker system relayed messages from a command centre at Nantwich. In the event of an emergency, staff would have been required to stay underground. Emergency beds and rations for the staff were stored in the lower tunnel. The food was replaced about every 16 months. The planned guard rooms were never utilised. Guardian was not used by Government as a storage point - it was too damp!

EXCHANGE CLOSED

After Guardian had been de-classified it continued to operate as a telephone exchange with around 40 staff. In 1985 the exchange closed, as its Strowger equipment became out of date with the new systems being available. This was superseded by 'System X and System Y' digital equipment. With the introduction of the new technology, the Power 24 rota of 24 hour manning came to an end. As technology advanced, fibre-optic cables were installed in the tunnels.

A vehicle known to staff as 'the tractor', pulled the heavy cables down the tunnels. Powered by batteries, it had metal wheels, and one seat for the driver. It travelled at slow speed and became virtually redundant with the introduction of the much lighter fibre-optic cables.

Staff often used bikes to go through the tunnels. There had also been a rule that they should walk in pairs because it was so disorientating if the lights went out in the pitch blackness.

The colour photographs on this and the following pages were taken about the time of the closure of the exchange.

OTHER TUNNELS ?

There has been mention of other tunnels from Guardian such as, to repeater stations at Stockport and Swinton, and also to an office block on London Road and the MRI. Others talk about a way in from Piccadilly Gardens. One ex-employee remembers seeing evidence of a covered-over tunnel at the Ardwick end. There was a tunnel towards Ardwick, and another to New Brown Street which were backfilled after construction of the main network. BT carried out test bores for a route to Stockport, but no further work was done. There were no other ways into Guardian as this would have compromised the safety and security of the complex.

237

Artesian wells

Artesian well under construction

There were three artesian wells below Guardian. One was under the premises of Alexander, Drew and Sons, 33 George Street, and another at 49-55 George Street on Post Office land. A third well was trialled but never used. Only one was in general use for cooling plant, cooling the premises and for emergency drinking water.

After the Abbeystead disaster in 1984, it was decided that a methane detection system was needed in Guardian. It was sited over the head of the artesian well, as this was the most likely point where gas could enter the tunnels. The well was a further 180ft below, although it was naturally contaminated, and could not be used. It had been contaminated with marl - a fine brown clay, which clogged the pipes.

A black liquid had been coming into the cable tube via the sump pumps at Ardwick. Tests identified it as pyrolusite, the main constituent of manganese dioxide. It had entered the system in the water directly under the Manchester University science labs, and it was initially believed this was the source. However, it was later thought that pyrolusite was a natural substance on site. The liquid could cause irritation to the eyes and throat, and so respirators, goggles and other protective gear was worn when maintaining the pumps in the workshop.

Ten sumps, each with two pumps ran constantly to take the incoming water to the City sewers or into the River Irwell. One pump was for normal use and the other in case the first pump failed. When this happened, an alarm was sounded and a visual indication was displayed on a panel. The faulty pump was repaired at the workshop. The pumps at Dial and Irwell House caused the forma-tion of a sandbank through the emission of water from

the Salford section in the river Irwell. Discharging into the river is done by agreement with the NWWA. In the rest of the Guardian complex, the water is sent into the sewer system. As Guardian is 75ft below the water table, around 17 million gallons of water seeps into the tunnel each year.

Although it has been previously stated that Guardian used the same artesian well as Boddingtons Brewery, I have learned from ex-employees at Guardian that this is not true.

Auto-start engine

This engine started automatically if there was a mains failure. When the output voltage, the frequency and speed were correct the engine's output automatically switched to all the essential equipment in Guardian. This included power plants feeding automatic-telephone equipment and transmission, and strategic lighting and sump pumps.

The other marine engines were started manually by means of compressed air. Non-essential equipment was powered by the two manual start engines and manual switching on the MV board in the engine room. In the photograph above, the starter batteries are seen on the right-hand side. At the back, behind the step ladders, is the compressed-air bottle used for starting one of the Crossley marine engines.

Corridor from the engine room

The pipes on the left are mainly from the auto-cooling equipment, and on the right are the exhaust pipes from the emergency engines. To combat the threat from Legionnaire's Disease, tablets of chlorine were added to the bottom of the cooling towers.

In the hoist bay, the hook from the crane can just be seen above the metal cabinet. The pipes on the left were foam inlets, and for carrying kitchen and toilet waste to the sewers. The wooden shut-off doors were fitted to close automatically when the fire alarm was activated.

Compressors for recharging start bottles

The exhaust went from the engines up a shaft and into the atmosphere above George Street.

The three engines are to the left, with the auto-start engine furthest away. On the right are the two compressors, with the Medium Voltage switching panels further down.

Close-up of the MV panels in the Engine room

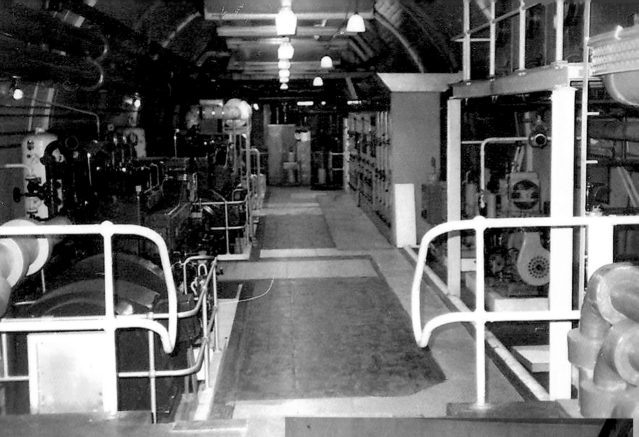

Engine room

The foul air extract point
could be best likened to a
huge concrete cone lying
on its side, and into which
foul air was channelled.
It was assisted by 10%
fresh air which pushed
it through a shaft and out
into the atmosphere. There
were six extract and intake
fans which circulated air
around Guardian.

There were portcullises at George Street and Rutherford House. Along with the 40 ton horizontal slab over the hoist bay, they could be closed off in an emergency. 'Guardian' was completely self-contained and could function for a few months with water facilities, engines, air recycling systems, food supplies and sanitation.

A bank of filters, which was the first stage of cleaning the air coming into the complex. The filters were changed periodically, and the individual sections pulled out, the dirty filter material removed and new material fitted. The material was supplied in rolls and had the appearance of a cotton wool-type fabric. There were many individual sections, so only a number at a time were replaced. It would have been too expensive to change the whole bank of filters each routine and very time-consuming. After this first stage of filtering, high-voltage wires created an electrical field that 'zapped' any particles that had found their way through the filter material. Moisture could be added to the air or taken out, depending on the conditions. Equipment rooms were maintained at a temperature of about 70°F.

The tube or corridor known as 'Shaft 6'

Hoist bay showing moveable slab in the down position. The slab weighed over 40 tons, and would help seal the complex. To add to security, a horizontal metal shutter was later installed over the shaft.

Above: Hoist bay, below: engine room

Condensors for
the engines, and
air-conditioning

Workshops

The Test Desk

On the right is the MDF - main distribution frame,
and through the doors at the rear was the old analogue
telephone exchange with wall-to-wall uniselectors.
It was maintained by 15 technicians. When it was in
full operation it made a huge noise, but later when it
was used much less, it was possible to track a telephone
call by watching the uni-selectors operate.

The generator engines, made in Openshawe, were the same as those used on the Mersey Ferry boats. It has been claimed there were extraction problems. This was probably due to the official policy of only briefly testing standby engines, in order to save fuel. The various switch-on routines were carried out, annually, to start the engine and then it was shut down almost immediately. The lack of use would cause deposits to settle in the exhaust pipes, creating clouds of smoke. Above and to the left of 'Jane' are ten hooks. There were ten functions to be carried out before the engine fired, such as priming the bearings with oil. Each one of these stages was represented by a red disk which would be placed on the hooks when completed. It is thought that this and the other two engines were named after the curvaceous film stars by planners before they were installed in Guardian. One of the engines was later removed for health and safety reasons.

Opposite: The 500ft long equipment room with the 50V auto T8 telephone exchange. Further down are the rows of uniselectors.

Landing and access ladder, used when
lifts were broken or being serviced.

Underground Dwellings

DR SANDRA HAYTON

Byrom Street

'The undeserving poor attracted many labels; the dangerous class, the submerged class, the underclass.'

Two of the principal social consequences of the industrialisation of Britain were the breaking of the ties that had bound the village community and the growth of towns. The population of England and Wales grew from 9 million in 1801 to 18 million in 1851[1]. By 1851 54% of the population lived in towns compared to only 20% in 1800. The population of Manchester increased from 75,000 in 1801 to 303,000 in 1851.

The dramatic change in society was both unplanned and unprecedented. It brought feelings of shock, horror, amazement, curiosity and fear. Great masses of humanity were herded together often out of sight owing deference to no one. The good example of their betters had been removed as the elites fled the smoke and filth of the towns. The elites' previous attitude of charitable concern had been severely eroded by the passing of the New Poor Law in 1834 because 'where private charity created a moral bond between giver and recipient public relief dissolved that bond' [2]. The concern of the past was replaced by a love/hate relationship. The masses were needed to man the mills and factories, yet they brought in their wake disease and civil unrest. Furthermore they posed a clear potential threat to profits with their

252

demands on Poor Law Relief. Such feelings were most strongly felt in the North West of England.

Contemporaries were intrigued and alarmed by the changes in their society. Seeking an explanation their spotlight fell on the new phenomenon: the urban poor. Their focus centred on the vulgar upstart city of Manchester - the creation of this new social order.

The urban poor were perceived as falling into two distinct groups - the deserving poor and the undeserving poor. The undeserving poor attracted many labels: the dangerous class, the submerged class, the underclass. Whatever the epithet, decent society believed that this mass of humanity was growing rapidly. Their moral and physical degeneration would spread, enveloping not only the deserving poor and the honest working man, but in time, respectable society itself would be threatened.

Top: Camp Street 1944
Above: Watson Street

253

Byrom Street

'Robert Southey was so
alarmed and appalled
by what he saw
he declared that
he would rather be
hanged in London
than die a natural death
of a poor man
in Manchester'

Manchester's growing reputation as Shock City attracted visitors from far and wide. Some came to wonder at the magnificent multi-storey gas-lit mills in Ancoats. Others sought out the dark and dangerous world of the under-class. As early as 1808 Robert Southey was so alarmed and appalled by what he saw he declared that he would rather be hanged in London than die a natural death of a poor man in Manchester.(3) In 1836 Peter Gaskell described the people of the underclass as the uncultivated children of nature, who lived brutalised lives that contained a high degree of promiscuity (4).

Nationally, fear and concern were growing, perhaps spurred on by the visitation of cholera to Manchester in 1832, the trade depression of the 1840s and 'trouble on the continent'. Two comprehensive investigations were undertaken. Firstly, the National Inquiry into the State of the Populous Districts of England and Wales and secondly, a survey undertaken by the Morning Chronicle Newspaper.

254

In the early 1840s Dr Lyon Playfair was appointed Her Majesty's Commissioner to conduct the Inquiry into the towns of Lancashire (5). He reported on the dwellings of the poor and he noted what he described as a Lancastrian phenomenon: cellar dwellings. He reported that some of these dwellings had become lodging houses and thus represented the Black Hole of Calcutta (6). Playfair numbered the cellar dwellings in Manchester to be 4443, with a computed population of 18,217 in a town where, for example in the St George's area, 7095 people shared 33 petties or necessaries - (lavatories) 'many of which were unfit for purpose'. The nightsoilman, an evil necessity, left streets filthy and stinking and with effluvia pouring down especially in low-class areas. Playfair concluded his report by demanding concerned legislation to remedy the evil.

Angus Bethan Reach reported on the Manufacturing Districts for the Morning Chronicle Survey 1849 - 51. He noted that the better classes had removed themselves from the smoke and smells. Reach perceived Manchester as a magnet which attracted tramps and vagabonds who were usually incapable of field work and in poor health. Unlike many other reporters on the contemporary scene Reach took to the streets of Manchester and he met some very interesting characters. One such was 'a young boy with deep-sunk eyes and a square bony jaw with a vile expression who walked Market Street at night often in partnership with a woman' (7). Reach maintained that many of the people that he encountered found shelter in conditions worst than those provided for the pauper and the criminal.

To demonstrate his point Reach entered such shelters. He visited a lodging cellar. The first room he entered measured 12ft by 8ft and neither Reach nor his companion could stand without stooping. The cellar

'The nightsoilman, an evil necessity, left streets filthy and stinking and with effluvia pouring down especially in low-class areas'

contained about 12 men, women and children and at least 6 other residents were absent at the time of the visit. All the inhabitants slept together on the straw-strewn stone floor. The back cellar was used for match making. Two young children slept on the shavings. All the residents of this cellar were natives of Co. Mayo, Ireland.

Reach and his companion then visited the worst cellar in Manchester. They were deeply shocked by what met their eyes - 'we proceeded into the inner cellar. They were literally vaults, three of them opening one from another. The air was thick with damp and stench. The vaults were mere subterranean holes utterly without light. The flicker of the candle showed their grimy walls reeking with foetid damp which trickled in greasy drops to the floor. Beds were huddled in every corner. In one bed a man was lying fully dressed and beside him slept a well-grown calf in the next cellar. Two boys were sleeping in one bed and beside them slept an old man (who was) stark naked and black with filth'. Reach ended by declaring himself glad when he found himself breathing the comparatively fresh air 'as could be found in Angel Meadow' (8)

The National Enquiry into Towns and The Morning Chronicle survey were not the only respectable publications to condemn cellar dwellings. The Builder in 1844

Below Top: Bridgewater Street

Below: Cellar shop

256

reported that a great proportion of inhabited cellars were dark, damp, ill ventilated and dirty. Moreover, such dwellings were morally evil and the paper's correspondent questioned whether an underground hole 12ft by 15ft square could possibly be suitable for human habitation.

Peter Gaskell, a doctor who lived for a short period in Manchester, reported that cellars housed the lowest of all classes and were places that were the very picture of loathsomeness, which quickly became the disgusting receptacles of every species of vermin that could infest the human body (9). Other reporters claimed that such dwellings resembled a putrid carcass filled with maggots and that they were fit for toads and toads only. Anthony S Wohl in his book Endangered Lives writes that, in the eyes of respectable Victorians, the inhabitants of cellars were 'regarded as a sub-species of cave dweller, scarcely human, a form of low life, a tribe of troglodytes and human moles' (10)

Collyhurst

Census returns frequently designate specific addresses as having a cellar dwelling. Research by way of contemporary maps together with census returns, principally for 1861 and 1871,indicates that cellar dwellings were to be found on main thoroughfares, down dark alleys in closed courts and under back-to-back houses. Sanitary reformers roundly condemned both closed court and back-to-back constructions as they severely limited ventilation and light to the houses. The cellar underneath such a house would be even less enviable. Maps indicate the presence of cellars by a flight of steps leading either up to a front door or down to the cellar. However the number of flights on some maps did

'Other reporters claimed that such dwellings resembled a putrid carcass filled with maggots and that they were fit for toads and toads only.'

not equate to the number of designated cellar dwellings in that particular street according to the census return. It was possible that entrance to the cellar was gained via the house above, but more probably the cellar did not have a separate door. Entrance and exit was by means of a window type arrangement at street level.

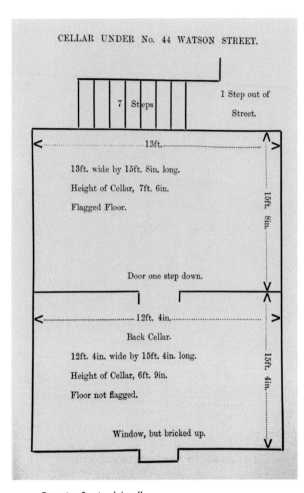

CELLAR UNDER No. 44 WATSON STREET.

7 Steps

1 Step out of Street.

13ft.

13ft. wide by 15ft. 8in. long.

Height of Cellar, 7ft. 6in.

Flagged Floor.

15ft. 8in.

Door one step down.

12ft. 4in.

Back Cellar.

12ft. 4in. wide by 15ft. 4in. long.

Height of Cellar, 6ft. 9in.

Floor not flagged.

15ft. 4in.

Window, but bricked up.

Detective Caminada's cellar dwelling diagram

Nassau Senior, a contemporary and supporter of Edwin Chadwick, the sanitary reformer, observed house building in Manchester. He reported that in one place 'we found a whole street following the course of a ditch because in this way deeper cellars could be secured without the cost of digging, cellars not for storing goods or rubbish, but for dwellings for human beings' (11). Clearly such place would have been at the best damp at worst oozing, vermin-filled, stinking hotbeds of fever and utterly loathsome.

Clearly there were cellars and cellars. Indeed when the elites left the town centre their once grand houses could have become multiple occupancies. However the census returns do not indicate any cellar dwellers under such homes. A cellar or more correctly a basement under a once grand house, was intended for people to be in, whereas cellars were, as Nassau Senior suggested, intended for storage. Mrs Gaskell, in her novel Mary Barton draws a clear distinction between the squalid cellar home of the Davenports and the warmth and comfort of that of Alice Wilson. It has proved impossible to physically measure any designated cellar dwelling. Most of the buildings have been demolished. Of those that do remain, street levels have been raised, area steps have been removed and internal inspection is not always welcomed or sought.

Dunville Street, off Lower Byrom Street, Castlefield

Fortunately Jerome Caminada (12), a detective with the Manchester police force, provides a contemporary and perhaps the most definitive diagram of a cellar dwelling interior under two back-to back houses in Watson Street and Back Coopers Street Caminada's cellar had 8 steps down from street level, which would be approximately six ft. The first room measured 13ft x l5ft 8ins. The ceiling height was 7ft 6ins and the floor of the room was flagged. The back cellar was one further step down and measured 12ft 6ins x 15ft 4ins. The ceiling height was 6ft 9ins and the floor was not flagged. Caminada shows that the window in this back room was bricked up. He does not mention a window in the front cellar but the exterior photograph does show the presence of a window. The area steps from the street and the window would clearly have increased both light and ventilation to the cellar dwelling. The luxury of space and air found in the Watson Street cellar does not hold for many other cellar dwellings.

'...such place would have been at the best damp at worst oozing, vermin-filled, stinking hot beds of fever and utterly loathsome.'

259

Back alley Grove Street
and St John's Place

Numerous cellar dwellings were found in the St George's district of Manchester which contained the infamous 'Angel Meadow' visited by Reach. In the Old Mount the houses were of back-to-back construction, one room above another. Measuring externally by using map scales it is estimated that the houses were between 8ft and 9ft square. The 1861 census shows that there was a cellar dwelling under each house. One such cellar was home to John Bradley, his wife and family. John was an Irish born handloom weaver aged 60. His wife was a cotton winder, probably helping her husband. They had three children living with them, Elizabeth 20, who was a power loom weaver and sons Michael 19 and Thomas, 17, both of whom were hookers in a warehouse. The rent for the cellared room was l/- per week.

In Grove Street in the Deansgate district there were 27 cellar dwellings, one under each house. Each cellar is shown as having a flight of steps. The external estimated size was 22ft 7ins x14ft 3ins which was probably divided into two rooms. Each one of these cellar dwellings was far superior to those in the Old Mount but significantly smaller than Watson Street, even though the rents were almost identical.

The vast majority of designated cellar dwellings were without a regular supply of clean water. Contemporary maps occasionally show the presence of a pump within the court. Clearly the rent would reflect this convenience even if the supply was not always of the highest quality and regularity. Cellar dwellings would also be devoid of 'necessaries' and it has been claimed that more than 20 families were forced to share one privy. Little wonder that Dr John Leigh, Manchester's first Medical Officer of Health, wrote in 1868 'when we consider that even the air which finds access to these sunken habitations is obtained from the level of sewer openings and that in many instances, the invigorating rays of the sun can never reach their interiors, it can excite no surprise that the blanched and flabby children of which they are the homes, grow up into the stunted men and women that crowd the streets of the manufacturing towns'. (13)

The underclass were seen as a huge mass of humanity living lives that were filled with drunkenness, immorality, licentiousness and brutality. Cellar dwellers were, as Wohl described, similarly almost subhuman and a race apart. For Engels the main constituent part of the underclass was the 'wild barbaric tribe from across the water' - the Irish. Patrick Carney and his family epitomise the picture of the underclass painted by many contemporary observers. He was head of a cellared household in Ludgate Hill in the Angel Meadow area. Patrick had been born in Ireland as had his 28-year old wife. Patrick was a barrel dealer and his wife was a hawker. They had two Manchester born children. Patrick's Irish born mother-in-law aged 50 and his brother-in-law, 17 shared the cellar as did two Irish born lodgers, John Knowsley, 60 a hawker and Mary Barnett 46, a charwoman. Clearly this cellar was indecently overcrowded. To conform to decency standards there had to be separate sleeping arrangements for non-married adults. However, the

'...it can excite no surprise that the blanched and flabby children of which they are the homes, grow up into the stunted men and women that crowd the streets of the manufacturing towns.'

The only entrance into a cellar dwelling

Carney family is not typical of cellar dwellers across Manchester. In the most Irish area, St George's 41% of cellar dwellers were born in Manchester, 44.3% in Ireland. Across Manchester as a whole in 1861 only 29% of cellar dwellers were born in Ireland.

Occupations such as dealers and hawkers etc have been described as 'penny capitalism' and around 29% of all working cellar dwellers in 1861 followed similar trades. In 1851 Elizabeth Wild and her husband lived in a house with their four children on Oldham Road. By 1861 she was still living on Oldham Road, but now in a cellar. Between 1851 and 1861 she had given birth to another child. The 1861 census suggests that one of the other children has died. To feed and clothe the family and pay the rent Elizabeth had become a herb dealer. Ten years later she is still in the same cellar and describes herself as a herbalist. Two other children are still at home and she also provides a home for her two grandchildren. In 1871 the rent for the cellar was 2/3d. Many cellar dwellings were female-headed and of these in 1861 approximately 83% were widowed.

A cellared dwelling may have been a small step up the ladder for Agnes Wallace. In 1861 she and her three children aged 8,7 and 5 were inmates in Salford Workhouse. Agnes was 27 and she was widowed. She gave her occupation as a hand silk winder, a trade that was in severe decline. In 1871 Agnes and the children are living in a cellar in Wright's Street in the Deansgate area of the town. She has found more secure employment in a cotton mill. Despite still being a widow she is shown on the census as the mother of four more children. By 1881 she has progressed even further up the housing ladder and is living in a house in Pendleton, Salford. Three of the four extra children are at home. It is very likely that the other child have died.

Back Irk Street

Life for many cellar-dwelling children was short. It has been estimated that 1 in 2 failed to reach their 5th birthday. Medical Officer of Health returns listing the causes of death amongst the under 5s include smallpox, whooping cough, diarrhoea, bronchitis, pneumonia, even teething, all of which took a heavy toll on the general under-5 population. The impact upon the children living in damp and foul holes in the ground would have been even more profound.

A further threat to the life of such young children was the use of Godfrey's Cordial - opium. It was a sleeping draught and was especially favoured by the 'nurse' who cared for the babies of working mothers. The cordial was so popular that the resultant deaths were described as the 'slaughter of the innocents'. The recorded cause of death in such cases was given as 'failed to thrive'.

Whenever a society perceives itself to be under threat it seeks someone or something to blame. Victorian society certainly felt fearful and helpless in the face of the dramatic changes brought upon their society emanating

'A further threat to the life of such young children was the use of Godfrey's Cordial - opium. It was a sleeping draught and was especially favoured by the 'nurse' who cared for the babies of working mothers.'

Grove Street

from the massive increase in the population in their town. The town's very heart was now inhabited by a mass of people who were a race apart, both in appearance and behaviour, many of whom lived in greatly overcrowded holes in the ground out of sight, and perhaps more importantly, out of control. Society's fears were regularly stoked by articles suggesting that the hatching of plots and the practice of the most shameful vices were every-day occurrences in these dens. The vast majority of cellars were rightly condemned. Attempts were made to prohibit cellars being used as dwellings by the passing of Local Improvement Acts, but without alternative habitation the cellars remained. It took decades for such places to disappear.

Sandra Hayton's great interest in cellar dwellings and their inhabitants can possibly be traced back to her childhood holidays at her aunt's boarding house in North Wales. The house had a huge cellar and descending the steps to the dark corners filled her with equal measures of fear and fascination.

Decades later, while working at Salford Local History Library, she noticed the occasional word 'cellar' written on census returns. Her childhood fascination returned and she wanted to know more about the people who lived in these dark spaces.

She spent over six years on a part-time degree course at Salford University finding answers to her questions, and her obsession with the cellar dwellers has remained.

References

1 Anthony S Wohl - *Endangered Lives* Methuen & Co. Ltd 1984 p4

2 Himmlefarb *The Idea of Poverty* Faber & Faber 1984 p150

3 R. Southey *Letters from England* ed. J Simmons Cresset Press Ltd (London) 1951

4 P Gaskell *Artisans and Machinery* second edition Frank Cass (London) 1968 p81

5 L Playfair - *Health in Towns* - Commissioned Report into the State of Large Towns in Lancashire - Printed by Clowes & Son Stamford St London 1845.

6 ibid p45

7 *Labour and the Poor of England & Wales 1849 -1851 Vol.1* ed. J Ginswick, Frank Cass 1983 p31&32

8 ibid p 78

9 Gaskell op cit p83

10 AS Wohl op cit p296

11 E Gauldie - *Cruel habitations* Alan & Unwin 1974 p84

12 J Caminada *25 years of Detective Life* John Heywood 1895 Vol 1

13 Simon & Inman *The Rebuilding of Manchester* Longmans (no date) p73

Use has also been made of other works by the author- *A Search for the Underclass* Lanes & Cheshire Antiquarian Society Vol 96 2000 Manchester Regional History Review 1998 Vol. Xll.

A Search for the Underclass Unpublished PhD Thesis 1995 Salford University.

Dangers and medals in the sewers

JIM MORTEN REMEMBERS

Above: 80ft below Mill Street c1970 with a Spire alarm

Below: Jim with director Yvonne Deutschman during the making of the BBC documentary 'The Sewermen' c1987

Jim Morten worked for the Council in Manchester for thirty-five years, starting in 1955. He was a sewer foreman in the town centre and also the Sewer Safety Officer in 1972. He was based at Pollard Street, then later Hooper Street.

Jim recalls that at Wadeson Road, off Brunswick Street, Ardwick, there were manholes cut into the red sandstone rock. In the Market Street sewer there were tunnels off it in the sandstone that went as far as Cannon Street. These were either filled or blocked off with the building of the Arndale Centre.

He also had memories of the sewers cut out of the sandstone under St Ann's Square. From a manhole in Market Place (now New Cathedral Street), it was possible to walk underground and see shelves in the rock.

Hazards down in the sewers included gas and a lack of oxygen, and so he always carried a Spire Alarm detector.

He had an interesting find in a sewer - an Americas Cup medal commemorating the efforts of the crew of the boat owned by Sir Thomas Lipton, the tea tycoon. Lipton made five unsuccessful attempts between 1899 and 1930 to win the prestigious sailing race, each time in boats not so luckily named 'Shamrock'. Americans, impressed by Lipton's sporting attitude and determination, presented him with a gold cup with the engraved inscription 'To possibly the World's worst yacht builder, but absolutely the World's most cheerful loser'. Jim has since lost the medal.

He was always alert to the potential dangers, especially in sewers like 'Work 6', which was 80ft deep and close

Below & opposite bottom:
The tumbling Bay, under Fairfield Street

to Clayton Aniline, with dangers of gas, chemicals and flooding. His favourite tunnel was Market Street because it was easy to get through and always had something of interest to see.

Jim was once asked by a lady to look for a wedding ring she had inadvertently dropped down a grid on Peter Street, close to where she worked, near the Free Trade Hall. She had only been married for three weeks. He managed to find it and was rewarded with a kiss. He has kindly allowed me to reproduce items from his collection of news cuttings and photographs.

DANGERS FROM SEWER GASES.

CAUTION TO SOUGHERS.

The attention of the Paving, Sewering, and Highways Committee having been called to the carelessness of workmen, employed in the Sewering Department, in omitting, before entering shafts sunk in the ground, to first apply tests to ascertain whether or not there is any noxious gas or foul air therein, the Committee hereby direct that the Foremen and Leading Men must hereafter strictly observe the following rules, viz:- That before entering, or allowing other workmen to enter, any shafts of a depth of 10 feet and upwards in loosely filled up ground, and 20 feet and upwards in solid ground, lighted candles or shavings must be first lowered into the shafts, and if they do not burn brightly, owing to the existence of gas or foul air therein, the bellows or blow-george must be at once sent for and applied, and no one must be allowed to enter such shafts until the air therein has been thoroughly purified.

Town Hall, Manchester,
10th March, 1899.

BY ORDER OF THE COMMITTEE.

Left: Penstock, City Road

INDEX

ACKNOWLEDGMENTS

Harold Addie, Derek Barlow, Jim Beckett, Anthony Shelmerdine-Boskovic, Cliff Brierley, Paul Broadhurst, Neil Brunsden, Charley Coyle, Enid Cresswell, Colin Curtis, Graham Daniel, Lilian Docherty, Gary Dunkerley, Ron Edwards, Harry Fairhurst, Roger Fitzgerald, David George, Mrs Guard, Donald Henderson, Andy Haymes, Peter Hayward, David Hilton, Jane Hogg, David Holt, Ken Howarth, Terry Hull, Emily Hulley, Maurice Ireland, John Jocys, Chris Jones, Tony Kidd, Ray Lyons, Bob Magee, Kenneth May, Anthony Middleton, Joyce Moreton, Jim Morton, Frank Moss, Mark O'Brien, Steve Parle, Phil Patten, Steve Powell, Mike Russell senior & junior, Barbara Shaw, Chris Smythe, Jack Tempest, John Tranter, Ron Trulio, Ian Whyte, Bill Williamson, Ken Wilson, Tom Webster, Frank Wood and to anyone I may have inadvertently missed.

Arndale Centre Management, Boots Management, BT Archives, Caernarfon Record office, Coop Archives, Fairhurst Design Group Ltd, Glaxo Smith Kline, John Goodchild Collection, Greater Manchester County Record Office, Habitat, House of Fraser, Harrods Archives, Institution of Civil Engineers, Manchester Central Library Local Studies and Archives, Manchester Council Building Control, Manchester Council Legal Records, Manchester University Archives, Museum of Science and Industry, The National Archives, Printworks, Salford Local Studies Library, Science Museum, St Ann's Church, Trafford Local Studies Library, The Waterways Archive (Ellesmere Port).

With thanks to everyone who has contacted me, supplied photographs, or gave information at my talks.

Special thanks to proof readers Cynthia Hollingworth, Pat Gothard and Judith Warrender

Front Cover: 'Central Foundations' Photographer: Andrew Paul Brooks ©2008 Paul Brooks/Urbis. Commissioned by Urbis for the exhibition Reality Hack: Hidden Manchester, 2008. Images from Reality Hack: Hidden Manchester are available to purchase from www.andrewbrooksphotography.com

Illustration page 163 top: a section of the lithograph 'Victoria Station 1848' by Arthur Fitzwilliam Tait (1819-1905) by kind permission of the Science Museum/Science & Society Picture library

Photograph pages 212-213 by kind permission of Popperfoto/Getty Images
Photograph page 169 by kind permission of simplonpc.uk

Select bibliography
Life Sentence - the Memoirs of Hartley Shawcross, Constable 1995.
The Canals of Northwest England, Hadfield and Biddle, David & Charles 1970
A Pictorial history of the Mersey and Irwell Navigation, John Corbridge, EJ Morten 1979
A Century in Co-operative Insurance, Ronald Garnett, George Allen & Unwin Ltd 1968
Roman Manchester, Charles Roeder, 1900
The Tubular Life-Boats 1850-1939, Grahame Farr, Papers on Life-Boat History, no 4, 1977

Various editions - City News, Daily Dispatch, Guardian, Manchester Courier, Manchester Evening Chronicle, Manchester Evening News